VENUS
unbound

A Guide to

Actualizing

the Power of

Being Female

DINA VON ZWECK
and JAYE SMITH

A Fireside Book

Published by Simon & Schuster

New York • London • Toronto • Sydney • Tokyo

Fireside

Simon & Schuster Building
Rockefeller Center
1230 Avenue of the Americas
New York, New York 10020

FIRESIDE and colophon are registered trademarks
of Simon & Schuster Inc.

Designed by Chris Welch
Manufactured in the United States of America

10 9 8 7 6 5 4 3 2 1

Library of Congress Cataloging in Publication Data

von Zweck, Dina.
    Venus unbound.

    "A Fireside book."
    1. Women—Psychology.   2. Femininity (Psychology)
3. Self-perception.   4. Self-actualization (Psychology)
I. Smith, Jaye.   II. Title.
HQ1206.V66   1989   155.6'33   89-16792

ISBN 0-671-68074-9

Acknowledgment

Malaika Adero's professional expertise and radiant presence guided this book through its many stages at Simon & Schuster. In appreciation, a fond thank you.

Based on the
Feminine Enhancement ™ Workshops

A new way of entitlement
and empowerment for every woman

To Marlene Connor, literary agent and friend—a special thanks for your insight, encouragement, and generosity of spirit.

Table of Contents

Table of Contents

Preface

Venus Unbound provides you with something that no other book can: a means of seeing who you really are, the opportunity to experience the beauty of your Inner Feminine Power, and practical ways of using your power in day-to-day life.

This book is based on the series of Feminine Enhancement™ Workshops that we hold throughout the year. Women of all ages and attitudes have participated in this reunion with their Inner Feminine Power. Each participant's experience is unique, their responses very different. But they all come away from the workshops with a sense of renewed vitality, with feelings and practical ideas about how their energy can be directed. When we first started, we saw the workshops as just a good idea. But over time they've become much more than that. The emotional rewards of being with women who are experiencing their own true nature for the first time and feeling the power within are extraordinary for us.

There's no doubt that women have gained power in the workplace, in the marketplace, and at home. Joining together in group efforts has helped us make progress. And as we sit back and assess our job, family, love life, children, and paycheck, we can get a better understanding of just how this progress directly affects us. We have more of a say in managing our lives. By establishing a collective agenda, we've freed ourselves from many unnecessary constraints. But still, there's something missing.

A mass movement can be enormously effective in producing change for women. It requires, however, that women have a common ground and a commonality of experience. The next step is to look at the uniqueness of each individual woman and find the special attributes and qualities that will lead her to positive self-change and growth.

We're now beginning to find out just how unique we are, individually, as women—and we're finding out that you can't put femininity under one umbrella any more than you can put love in a basket. You have your way, your path . . . and what is right for you is not necessarily right for someone else.

A bird's-eye view of *Venus Unbound* can be found in the table of contents. This book is an expanded version of a program that has meant a lot to many women. After our own experiences in presenting the workshops, it is a labor of love to make this material available to a larger audience.

We start each workshop with an invocation, joining hands in a circle. Unite with us now in reading this affirmation, together with thousands of women who, like yourself, want to reclaim the Inner Feminine Power they were born with.

"Each one of us is unique, and each one of us is guided on her own life path. We are here today to discover and define ourselves in new ways . . . and to support each other's individual quest."

Introduction

What do women *really* want after they have it all—career, success, marriage, and motherhood? They want to feel "feminine."

For many women, femininity is something you buy: seductive shoes, a crisp black taffeta dress, lustrous pink-orchid lipstick, and antiaging lotions that promise beauty. Or it's something you do: diet faithfully, run rigorously, and have a meaningful relationship.

After years of trying hard to become a "new woman" who has it all, most women still think something's missing. They still don't feel entirely comfortable with themselves. And they're taking time out to ask themselves, "Why don't I *feel* feminine?"

The simple answer is that the majority of women in today's society have lost a strong and important connection to their authentic femininity. This *true* femininity is not a product of our consumer culture, nor is it an attitude or state of mind. Femininity is a *process*, and being feminine means different things at different times.

Confusing? You bet! Many different feminine attributes exist inside us at the same time. They are like inner voices which

Introduction

sometimes work in harmony and sometimes at cross-purposes. If they rule you, they can become "authorities" that keep you from actualizing your full potential and meeting your day-to-day needs. But if you learn to recognize and understand these different attributes inside you, you will also be able to activate their powers whenever you need them. Then, instead of becoming authorities that rule you, they become inner feminine guides that can help you.

We've named the feminine guides Eva, Kendra, Nixa, Belinda, Diana, and Erika. They are images of who you are and what you can become, and they need to be evoked and listened to so that you can see just how rich, complex, and powerful you really are.

The feminine guides are based on a deep understanding of the six most important guiding forces in every woman. The concept is original and fresh, but the wisdom it embodies goes back through the ages. Like all good innovative ideas, this one is simple—and extremely useful.

Being truly feminine means being alive and awake so you can listen to your guides, because what they tell you will empower and enliven your whole feminine self. But remember, your own femininity is unique—the way you love, work, create, nurture, grow, and live is special to your particular heart, mind, and body.

In this book you will learn to say yes to many different parts of yourself. And you'll learn to purposefully direct and use your Inner Feminine Power in practical and concrete ways. As you focus on bringing your powers into play in everyday life, everything will become clearer, more vibrant, and more satisfying.

Venus Unbound was created for every woman who wants to go into the twenty-first century with new views about what it feels like to be feminine, from her own perspective and without being manipulated by cultural values. By gaining access to your *real* voice and your *real* experience, you will be able to say, "This is who I am. This is what I value."

Once you are fully in touch with your own life-giving energy, fears and doubts dissolve, depression lifts, anger dissipates—and you will come to know and value what is truly important to you. The inner guides will open the doors to courage, creativity, love, self-confidence, spontaneity, and imagination. They will mirror your own capacity for loyalty, resilience, clear thinking, solitude,

Introduction

wisdom, and steadfastness. You have the ability to tap inner resources so that they become uniquely alive and usable. Your deepest wishes can be expressed and lived, and you can relate and respond to others with loving concern. You will recognize and value the innate energy that contributes to your own personal growth and enables you to reach out to others.

There are eleven chapters in this book—in each chapter you will take another step on the path toward Inner Feminine Unity. As you make your way through the book, the rich patterns and beauty of your deep inner self will become more and more apparent to you. As your own special way opens and you move forward into the new dimension of your authentic self, your Inner Feminine Power will grow stronger. You will become wiser in all the things that matter to *you*. No matter how conventional or unconventional you are, no matter how strong or weak you think you are, and no matter how feminine or unfeminine you now see yourself as being, this book will give you a very special opportunity to open up a new world of possibilities for self-development and for sharing all you truly are with others. Whatever is uniquely alive within you will be given a chance to surface in the many visualizations and in the exercises. You will experience your own alive energy and strength and—with the help of your Guides—get to know an authentic self that may now be hidden and dormant.

The book is designed for you—a woman who is bright, perceptive, and interested in actualizing her deepest, most powerful self. A self that is profound, although some parts may be covered over with layers of misconceptions about its own strength and beauty. Rather than digging up what is buried, *Venus Unbound* will allow the variegated parts of you as an individual to surface like silvery fish in a dark sea. They will glimmer and shine and show you patterns as they swim and dart before your eyes. Similarly, the book will provide you with everything you need to be able to see what was previously inaccessible.

The way opens . . . begin at your own pace. Take time with everything. There is no need to rush. Be mindful. Prepare yourself by making a commitment to remain open and receptive to the organizing force behind your true self—your Inner Feminine Power.

p a r t

1

Everything you encounter in this book will be easily accessible because the material has been designed to take you from step-by-step preparation all the way to actualizing your full Inner Feminine Power. Obviously it is not something you can do overnight, but the time you spend will be rewarding. Part One starts by putting you on the path toward feminine unity and ends with love messages from your Guides. In between this beginning and end, you will experience your own true nature in all its many aspects. We hope it will turn out to be a rewarding process of inner fulfillment.

To get started, reread the table of contents and familiarize yourself with the chapter titles. In that way, you can get an overall feeling for what's in store for you. Then read the text so that you establish a feeling relationship with the words, sentences, and paragraphs. Remember, go at your own pace. A mental understanding will produce results on the mental plane only. A feeling response is necessary here so that the results also work on the emotional plane.

Never attempt to go farther than you feel you are ready to. Practicing the visualizations, affirmations, and exercises can release enormous amounts of stored-up energy. Once this energy is at your disposal, it can be directed so that positive self-change can occur. Powerful forces are available to you in the first half of the book. They will work in your best interests if you use them *when you are ready*.

Remember, too, that it is sometimes necessary to counteract discouragement. Small progress, great progress, and even standstills occur in their own time, not ours. If things go slower than you'd hoped or obstructions stand in your way, concern yourself with maintaining an optimistic attitude. It is within your ability to focus on the positive present and future. In the words of the old song, "Accentuate the positive, eliminate the negative, and don't mess with Mr. In-Between." Latch on to the affirmative when you need to.

1

Twelve Steps Toward Feminine Unity

In the following chapters, you will be introduced to your Guides, and you will learn how to contact them directly and how to ask for what you want and need. You will learn how to accept the guidance necessary for your individual progress and self-growth. Knowing how to accept what is right for you at any given moment or situation is a major step toward self-realization.

In order to start working with your Guides at the highest level, a certain amount of clarity is necessary. Preparation for change is mostly a clearing-out process. Everything that will bog you down on your journey toward feminine wholeness must be thrown away. Anything that will prevent you from reclaiming your full feminine powers must be abandoned.

It's not as difficult as it sounds. Clearing your mind of outmoded precepts and putting yourself on the path to understanding is a step-by-step process. It is presented here in the Twelve Steps Toward Feminine Unity. There is no time limit or expectation of how long each step will take. For now it is enough to read this chapter and acquaint yourself with the twelve-step preparation process. Take in and digest as much as you need. When you are presented with a large pantry of food, you don't eat it all at once. You take what appeals to your appetite. So it is with the nourishment of the Inner Feminine. You can always return to this chapter; it will be there for you again and again.

While you are reading the Twelve Steps Toward Feminine Unity, remember to:

1. Remain centered.
2. Remain open and aware.
3. If your vision is not as clear as you would like, remember that the way will open. Have faith and trust.

By doing this, your mind will be uncluttered and you will be able to approach the steps at the highest level.

For each step you take, a feminine power is released. Taking Step One releases the Power of Trust. Taking Step Two releases the Power of Receptivity. Other steps release other powers. At the end of each step, you will learn what power you can now release. When you have completed Step One, you will read *"Release the Power of Trust."* After Step Two, you will read *"Release the Power of Receptivity."* As you go along, you will begin to recognize and feel the Inner Feminine Powers. And you will be able to link them directly to the steps you take.

Proceed at your own pace to read and take the twelve steps toward feminine unity.

Twelve Steps Toward Feminine Unity

1. Know and Believe

Know and believe that you already possess all you need to make use of your greatest feminine potential. The strength and power to make the most of your own unique nature resides in you *right now*. Your greatest capabilities and your wildest dreams can be fulfilled by activating your feminine energies, just as a match ignites wood. But the fire of your hopes and desires must be directed. A match can bring warmth and coziness to the fireplace. Tossed into a dry forest, however, it can cause devastation.

The quest for Inner Feminine Unity is a personal journey. It involves getting on the path and learning (over and over again) to listen to your own inner wisdom. The power to begin the journey and stay on the path resides within you. Know and believe that this power is enormously potent and can only be activated by you and you alone.

Whatever private convictions you may hold, trust that the power to change exists within you at this very moment. Whether your desires involve abundance and prosperity, peace and contentment, or happiness in love, know and believe that you can set this power in motion for the benefit of others and yourself.

Take the time to assure yourself of your own power. Affirm its strength. An affirmation is a simple positive statement that holds the truth. Repeating the affirmation emphasizes its truth and reinforces its validity. At this moment, say to yourself, silently or aloud: "I am my own power to create abundance, peace, and love."

Release the Power of Trust

2. Prepare Yourself

Prepare yourself for self-change and growth. Old clichés would have us compare this to planting a seed in a garden that is made ready. But this pat analogy doesn't come to terms with the invisible cities within. There may very well be peaceful places, but distractions, anxiety, fear, and uncertainty are also commonplace. Preparation, then, requires more than weeding and clearing out. It requires getting in touch with the Inner Feminine that can *always* prepare room for enrichment. A book can give you an excellent program and can set out possibilities for growth. It can inspire and stimulate. But it cannot do the necessary preparation. Only you can do that.

Begin by looking within. Search for a place inside yourself that is open to growth at all times. Look for it and find it. It is the abode of the Inner Feminine, a place where you can recharge and replenish yourself.

Self-change and *growth* are large abstract ideas. They can sound intimidating, especially if you are trying too hard to make things happen. Go slowly. There is no hurry. At this point, don't concern yourself with anything but reaching within to a place where progress is *always* furthered, the place of the Inner Feminine. Take time to search for and find that place.

There is a part of you that is always responsive to new possibilities. Sometimes it is difficult to be receptive to new growth—frustration, anger, lack of self-esteem, or depression often block the way. In spite of that, prepare yourself for positive self-change and growth. Anticipate and expect that good things will soon appear in your life, and receive them with open-mindedness when they do.

Prepare now to receive new growth and energy. Sit quietly and close your eyes. Feel yourself *preparing* for new possibilities. No action is necessary except to prepare yourself.

Release the Power of Receptivity

3. Acknowledge Yourself

Acknowledge yourself as you are today. At this very moment, accept who you are and smile upon yourself like sunshine on a flower. No matter what ups and downs you may be experiencing in your life, take time to recognize yourself as you would recognize a good friend that you haven't seen in a long time. Observe yourself in a kind and loving way, putting aside critical attitudes and narrow judgments.

Respect what's happening within yourself today. Obstructions, standstills, and progress are all necessary for your evolvement. If you feel you are not getting everything you want out of life, trust yourself. Things may come to fruition slowly. Remain centered and focused on the present moment.

Acknowledge your capacity to rise above limitations. Reach deep within. It is not a question of thinking or knowing that you have the power to free yourself from unnecessary constraints. It is a matter of *feeling* the power. Take the time to contact your inner reservoir of strength. Allow yourself to feel its power.

Begin to appreciate your inborn nature and the power that flows through you. Allow the power of your true nature to shed light on a part of your life that feels stagnant or unclear. Close your eyes and, for a moment, acknowledge the light within.

Acknowledge yourself not only for what you do, but for who you are. Unwind and relax. Be gentle with yourself. You can experience yourself in many different ways, but at the center there is a calm, tranquil core. And from it, energy radiates and animates your being. Take time to acknowledge your peaceful center and the power emanating from it.

Release the Power of Aliveness

4. Eliminate Fears and Doubts

Eliminate fears and doubts and cast them away as if throwing away chains. Untie every aspect of your life from restraining aspects.

Your fears and doubts—whatever they may be—keep you in a prison of your own making. You can dream in a prison, but you can't actualize your dreams. You can wish for freedom, but you are not free.

Begin with the self that knows and believes it possesses everything it needs, the self that is prepared for change, the self that acknowledges itself. This is the starting point. Go from here and begin to eliminate fears and doubts. Fear of loneliness, poverty, or illness, and doubts about your ability to attract love are all unnecessary constraints that confine and restrict feminine power. Despite what you may now think, fears and doubts *can* be eliminated completely from your life so that you can make new connections to your higher feminine self.

Fears and doubts clog channels to the Inner Feminine and interrupt or cut off energy. At this point, no action is necessary. It is enough to believe and feel that you can free yourself from fears and doubts.

To strengthen your belief, the following affirmation will be helpful. Saying it you yourself begins the process of letting go of all that is holding you back. The affirmation contains the truth—and saying it confirms its truth. Silently or aloud, affirm: "Fears and doubts, little by little, are cast away."

Release the Power of Tranquility

5. Be Generous

Be generous. Becoming ungrudgingly beneficent may seem difficult at first. But things get easier when you start with a perception of yourself. Remember that true perception comes from the heart, not the head. The mind is sometimes clouded, but the heart always speaks the truth. Listen to your heart.

Let your heart begin to tell you what and how you can give—and let it tell you what you must withhold for the present.

Being kind to those who hurt you, or giving freely to those in need, is not something that can take place overnight. Do not expect rapid progress. For now, it is enough to *feel* your own generous heart. Be generous with yourself first, allow yourself to listen.

Take the time to experience the power of a generous heart. Look within to a deep, and possibly secret, place where you do not love yourself. It may be an area that fills you with guilt or contempt. Or it may invite sadness. Bring your generous heart to that place. Be gentle with yourself. Befriend yourself. Give yourself all the warmth you need. Let the heart radiate light and eliminate darkness. Feel the effects of your generous heart.

Remember that this power is available to you wherever you go, whatever you do. And it can be used to benefit others as well.

It is said that we must first love ourselves before we can love others. It is easy to love good qualities. It is harder to love the hateful places. But that is exactly where generosity is most valuable.

Release the Power of the Heart

6. Discriminate

Distinguish between what furthers your well-being and what doesn't—and accept only nourishment that contributes to positive growth. When you sit down at the dinner table, you want it to be filled with appetizing food that will sustain you. If you sat down to a table and you were served garbage, you wouldn't accept it as your dinner. But sometimes we can be served verbal garbage and not even realize it. In family situations, subtly sarcastic or contemptuous comments can pass unnoticed. At work, manipulative power plays can be accepted as worthwhile.

But the point is not to look at situations and experiences with a cold, discerning eye. The idea is to see—with perception and intuition—what sustains and nurtures you. Penetrating inner vision enables you to separate the seeds from the chaff. And the ability to see beneath the surface of things is a skill you can cultivate. Your present awareness can be fine-tuned by simply using it. The more you look at what promotes growth and what doesn't, the keener your skill will become.

On a broader level, learning what furthers your well-being will enable you to go to true nourishment when you need it. In times of success, wealth and possessions may be the good fortune you need—or inner self-discipline and a generous heart may be more valuable.

To know and understand, and to discriminate between material success and inner success, is a sign of waking up to the Inner Feminine.

Watchfulness is all that is called for now. Look within—the sight within complements what can be seen on the surface.

Release the Power of Insight

7. Rejoice, Be Thankful, and Understand Your Path

Value and appreciate every moment of your life for what it is. Rejoice in communion and connectedness; understand that pain, sadness, blockages, and impediments are very necessary for personal growth and development; and be thankful that you can begin to see yourself on a path toward feminine wholeness. Start by rejoicing in some recent experience that was joyous and meaningful for you. *Feel* how this brings you in touch with the original experience again. Close your eyes and search for the feeling. Find it and stay with it for a few minutes.

Now, be thankful. Feel truly thankful for something that happened today. It can be even the most ordinary thing. Search for it and find it. Stay with the feeling.

Then (and here's the hard part) understand your path. It's a path you have chosen. While you may very well encounter unexpected events and situations, it is your path and it is your journey.

The journey is an inner quest for feminine unity, and the path is the way. Through your own choice, you are taking the steps.

Begin to take them with joy. Start your journey with thankfulness. Understand that the path and the journey and the joy and thankfulness are one. Close your eyes and bring them together. Feel that they are united. If they feel separate, slowly bring them closer and closer until they are one.

Release the Power of Joy

8. Stay in Touch with Your Fluid Feminine Nature

Your fluid feminine nature supports and carries you along, just as water can carry along a boat. Even if the boat has the most powerful engine available, it is the water that supports it—this is the nature of water. Be aware also of the upholding nature of the Inner Feminine. No matter how fast or slow you are progressing in your own personal growth, no matter what kinds of obstacles are in your way, take the time to feel that you are being buoyed up by something other than your own self-interests. Get in touch with the part of yourself that will hold you up whether you are speeding, or in low gear with your dims on, or at a complete standstill.

The Inner Feminine is flexible, and it will allow you to change course easily if you need to. The birth of a child, caring for an aging parent, or a career change all may require a change of plans. When you are in touch with your Inner Feminine, which is adaptable, pliant, and versatile, things have a tendency to flow smoothly. Problems that you've stockpiled don't seem so monumental.

Take time to *feel* the fluid nature of your Inner Feminine. Close your eyes and imagine that you are in a canoe at the edge of a tranquil lake. Paddle to the center of the lake. Now, put your paddle in the canoe and sit quietly. Feel how the water supports you. Take a moment to feel how the water effortlessly holds you up. Give in to the feeling and stay with it. Now use your paddle to return to shore.

Feel the support of your Inner Feminine. Give in to it. Let it support and carry you along.

Release the Power of Surrender

9. Be Aware of New Self-Growth and New Energies Being Liberated

When growth takes place and there is progress toward feminine unity and wholeness, energy is released. The amount of energy that is liberated is directly proportional to the amount of growth: the more growth, the more energy released. An enormous surge of energy usually occurs when major progress is made.

When inner rewiring takes place, old circuits are unplugged and discarded and new connections are made. Outmoded attitudes and outdated thinking is replaced by new—and more energetic— feelings and ideas. When you get rid of wiring that is obsolete, everything becomes clearer and your Inner Feminine can *see* what's what a lot better.

Think, for example, of a tree, which has more energy to grow to its full potential if its dead branches are clipped away. When a tree is pruned, the energy that previously went into maintaining the dead wood is released.

Be aware of your own feminine growth. Recognize it when it happens. Respect it. Trust it. Be mindful of just how far you have already traveled on your path, and remember your joys, triumphs, and hardships. Be mindful of the past and the future, while at the same time looking at your present new growth.

Begin to appreciate yourself. Commit your heart, mind, and body to giving yourself credit for who you *are*, not only for your accomplishments. Try to *feel* new growth instead of trying to define it. Whether your progress involves overcoming fears about old age, coming to terms with a relationship that is stagnating, or whatever, begin to experience growth. There can be pain or discomfort when dead wood is clipped away. There also can be doubts about how to see newly released energy. That's okay.

Keep alert to possibilities. Newly liberated energy can be extremely potent—whether it's concentrated and highly charged or diffused and mild. The smallest progress can sometimes free powers that are enormous when directed in the right way.

At this time there is nothing to do, nowhere to go. It is enough to witness and feel your own self-growth and the energies that are being liberated.

Release the Power of Observation

10. Protect Yourself from Injury to Your Inner Feminine

Harm to the Inner Feminine is not always apparent. Life's demands and conflicts can bruise the spirit in ways that are hidden from consciousness. Contempt, manipulation, and the withholding of affection are sometimes so subtle that they go unrecognized.

At other times, abuse of the Inner Feminine is identified for what it is—but it is accepted in order to maintain the status quo. In this case, there *is* an awareness, but it is accompanied by feelings of helplessness. If the harsh situation is allowed to continue, little by little, the power of the Inner Feminine is diminished. Like a searchlight that is constantly smudged by soot, after a while its ability to discover what it is searching for is curtailed.

Withdrawal is sometimes required to ward off injury to the Inner Feminine, while at other times, it may be necessary to take more decisive action. Withdrawal involves examining and exploring the nature of the injury and the damage it has done. In quiet contemplation, an assessment can be made by looking within. After that, no further action may be necessary.

If action is indicated, listen to your heart so that the movement forward can be made with love instead of rancor. Allow your Inner Feminine to protect you with a mantle of beauty. Proceed into the experience with high hopes. Protecting yourself from injury to your Inner Feminine releases new energies.

Release the Power of Beauty

11. Accept the Demands of Your Inner Feminine Self

Accept the demands of your Inner Feminine, and seize the opportunities it presents. It is important to differentiate between a demand and an opportunity. A demand is just that—it insists that you either satisfy it or take the consequences (which are usually severe). It is more than a request, because action must be taken. Awareness of the demands of the Inner Feminine must be addressed with complete honesty. Security and relationships, in this instance, are secondary.

An opportunity, on the other hand, is a chance—to make a new friendship, accept a job offer, etc. Some opportunities seem risk free, others can be challenging. It is the same with inner opportunities. In a new friendship, your Inner Feminine can give you the opportunity to be even more compassionate and loving, intuitive and trusting. Be open and aware of these inner opportunities, and when they arise, seize them. Take advantage of them and allow your feminine self to guide you.

In a new job, your Inner Feminine can give you the opportunity to assess your competitiveness or your flexibility. Remain receptive to what surfaces from within. A seemingly small opportunity sometimes opens many doors to feminine power.

And so it goes. When you accept external opportunities, the Inner Feminine can present you with equally important opportunities for inner growth. Be aware. Listen and look carefully at all the possibilities.

An opportunity is not necessarily the *right* set of circumstances in which progress *will* occur. You can only judge that after the fact. But when the chance for inner growth comes up in your life, it should be seized. To "seize the moment" means to embrace it, take hold of it and clasp it to you as something precious. Be mindful of the moments of inner opportunity, and recognize them when they occur.

Release the Power of Understanding

12. Have Courage. Reclaim Your Feminine Power

You were born with full feminine power. Through wrongheaded education and conformity to society's expectations, some of these powers have been lost and forgotten, misplaced along life's highway. You not only inherit genes, you also inherit a set of values which may or may not coincide with your own true nature. Family, friends, and lovers can mold your feminine self to their own expectations.

Frequently, people and institutions are limited themselves, and they want to pass on these limits so that conformity is achieved. They want to limit you to what *they* see as absolute truth. Fortunately, the Inner Feminine does not allow such a neat package. Our individual and collective powers break through every so often.

But this still does not permit a full spectrum of light. Half-light can illuminate dark corners and positive change can take place. However, the full radiance of feminine power can still remain intermittent and sometimes dim.

The last step toward feminine unity insists that you believe—in a feeling and heartfelt way (not just intellectually)—that you can reclaim the full feminine powers you were born with. This is the birthright of all women. For you, it means a union with powers that may have, for a long time, remained inactive.

For now, it is enough to feel that you *can* reclaim your feminine powers and direct them in a way that furthers your best interests.

Have courage. Allow yourself to feel that you are entitled to your birthright.

Release the Power of Unity

After you have read the steps, give yourself a breather. It's a lot to think about, isn't it? Well don't think about it too much. Thinking and acts of will are not needed immediately. It is enough for you to have a basic understanding of the path toward feminine unity and to put yourself on that path.

You are now ready to do a short visualization that will set you on your path. A visualization is a meditative exercise to help you get in touch with your true feelings, your intuition, and your insights. It's a relaxation technique that allows you to contact the inner self that you can't get in touch with at other times.

Putting Yourself on the Path

You can read the visualization into a tape recorder and play it back. If you decide to record this visualization and the others in the book, by the time you are finished you will have an excellent set of tapes. Since you will be listening to your own voice (rather than someone else's on a commercial tape), you will be doubly rewarded because you will hear your own self talking. Nothing could be better.

In this visualization, you will be putting yourself on the twelve-step path toward feminine unity. The visualization is called Putting Yourself on the Path.

Sit upright in a comfortable chair or cross-legged on the carpet. See that there are no distractions (unplug the telephone or turn on the answering machine). Start to feel at ease with the process of contacting your Inner Feminine. Begin the visualization (remember to pause briefly after each sentence and for a bit longer after each paragraph).

Putting Yourself on the Path

Close your eyes. Relax. Feel your body getting more and more relaxed. Feel your jaw loosening. Feel tension leaving your face.

Picture yourself in a dark woods. Walk around.
After a while you come to a round clearing. The sun has come out and there are flowers. Go through the clearing to the other side.

At the other side of the clearing, there is a path. You know instinctively that this is the way you want. Put yourself on the path. Notice your feelings. Are they happy? Afraid? Disinterested? Ashamed?

Begin to take a few steps on the path. Observe your stride forward. Is it hesitant? Lackadaisical? Notice your first steps.

Now you are ready to return to your everyday waking reality. Open your eyes. Stand up slowly and stretch.

After you have completed the visualization, take the time you need for quiet contemplation. Witness your feelings and thoughts. There is no hurry.

When you are ready, proceed to the next chapter and take the Femininity Assessment Quiz.

Summary

Below you will find a summary of the steps. The concise format will help you to see the Twelve Steps Toward Feminine Unity at a glance, and will help you begin your journey toward wholeness:

1. Know and believe that you already possess all you need to make use of your greatest feminine potential.

   ### *Release the Power of Trust*

2. Prepare yourself for change and growth by listening with awareness to your heart's guidance.

   ### *Release the Power of Receptivity*

3. Acknowledge and accept who you are at this very moment, and smile upon yourself like the sun on a flower.

   ### *Release the Power of Aliveness*

4. Eliminate fears and doubts by believing you can cast away constraints.

   ### *Release the Power of Tranquility*

5. Be generous. Begin by *feeling* the generous heart within you and opening it to the joy of giving.

Release the Power of the Heart

6. Discriminate between what furthers your well-being and what doesn't—and accept only nourishment that contributes to positive growth.

Release the Power of Insight

7. Rejoice, be thankful, and understand your path. Realize that everything you encounter on your path has value. Joy and appreciation as well as pain and suffering, each has its own worth in your self-development.

Release the Power of Joy

8. Stay in touch with your fluid feminine nature. The ebb and flow of its rhythms create balance and further progress.

Release the Power of Surrender

9. Be aware of new self-growth and new energies being liberated. Breakthroughs and contacts with your feminine powers require mindful attention.

Release the Power of Observation

10. Protect yourself from injury to your Inner Feminine. The right action can be determined by maintaining a watchful attitude.

Release the Power of Beauty

11. Accept the demands of your Inner Feminine and seize the opportunities it presents. Embrace a chance for self-growth and clasp it to you as something precious.

Release the Power of Understanding

12. Have courage. Reclaim your feminine power. Allow yourself to feel that you are entitled to power as your birthright.

Release the Power of Unity

2

~

Assessing Your Femininity

The six-part quiz in this chapter is designed to help you assess how you view your femininity. The purpose of the quiz is to put you in touch with your #1 Inner Feminine Guide, and with your Helping Guides.

There are no right or wrong answers. Your Guides are unique to *your* femininity, much the same as your body chemistry is unique to *your* body.

Read each question carefully and indicate your answer by checking the response that most closely mirrors your true feelings in each situation. When you are finished, turn to the scoring and evaluation section, where you will be introduced to your Guides.

SECTION ONE

	YES	SOMETIMES	NO
I think of myself as an outrageous flirt.			
Spending time to make my body alluring is important to me.			
I appreciate beauty and sexual pleasure more than work and success.			
I claim my sexual needs assertively.			
I have a taste for adventurous relationships.			
Fulfilling my desires and passion is easy for me.			
The way I move my body reveals the wisdom of pleasure.			
I am receptive to love and am hardly ever disappointed.			
It is during lovemaking that I can best communicate my femininity to my partner.			
Sex is love's most potent expression.			
I have an innate sense of beauty.			
Being sensuous is a fundamental way of life for me.			

SECTION TWO

	YES	SOMETIMES	NO
Setting goals and achieving them is second nature to me.			
Dealing with disappointment is a challenge.			
I feel like a woman of the world.			
Being objective is the most important way to look at life.			
I live according to reasonable plans.			
Fighting for my own needs and rights doesn't faze me.			
I was born to win.			
I set limits and manage time well.			
I get rid of old habits and patterns of behavior that have outlived their usefulness.			
My head rules my heart.			
In the workplace, my feelings are incidental to my goals.			
I like to schedule time with my partner rather than doing things on the spur of the moment.			

SECTION THREE

	YES	SOMETIMES	NO
I expect new experiences to be interesting.			
I love being full of creative ideas about everything.			
Being playful is part of my nature.			
I'm not afraid to take emotional risks like starting a new relationship or ending a friendship that's withered.			
I enjoy new projects that let me "play" with ideas and concepts.			
I feel curious about most everything.			
Adjusting to the unexpected isn't difficult for me.			
My life never feels cluttered.			
I act spontaneously—and my behavior is not grounded in conventionality.			
Innovative thinking interests me more than money.			
I operate by impulsive energy rather than concentrated willpower.			
I feel great when I can be highly imaginative.			

SECTION FOUR

	YES	SOMETIMES	NO
I would rather be an architect than a tour guide.			
I provide comfort and security to all those around me.			
A committed and monogamous love relationship is very important to me.			
I'm attuned to people's feelings, and I respond to their needs.			
Keeping my house tidy and organized gives me a feeling of satisfaction.			
In relationships, I am aware of my own tactfulness and timing, and I express feelings appropriate to the moment.			
It's natural for me to listen carefully to what others say.			
I have an innate ability to structure and order my environment.			
I am more attuned to the practical requirements of the moment than abstract ideas about the future.			
I could center my life around marriage and motherhood.			
"Nesting" and beautifying my home is a very pleasurable experience for me.			

SECTION FIVE

	YES	SOMETIMES	NO
I'm happiest when I'm alone, doing my own thing.			
I feel close to nature and untamed wilderness areas.			
A good relationship with a man is *not* limited to its sexual aspect.			
There are no "oughts" in my life.			
I feel independent and self-sufficient.			
I don't live by conventional beliefs, but rather by strong inner convictions.			
The approval of men is not necessary for my well-being.			
I dress to please myself rather than to impress others.			
I have an innate inclination for solitude.			
Walking in the woods by myself would give me great pleasure.			
Having time to myself—away from my partner—is important to me.			
Fully exploring what is happening or what has happened can only be done alone.			

SECTION SIX

	YES	SOMETIMES	NO
Feminine intuition is a most valuable form of intelligence.			
I have an uncanny sixth sense about the future.			
My wisdom and advice command respect from those around me.			
I feel an attunement with the phases of the moon and with seasonal cycles.			
Much of my life is mysterious and profound.			
It's easy for me to see straight to the heart of matters.			
I can understand what fate has in store for me.			
In close friendships with women, I recognize what is unique and special about each woman.			
I understand my "calling"—my reason for being here on earth.			
I am deeply connected to my inner healing powers.			
Intuition guides me in making sharp and wise judgments.			
I am never manipulated by flattery.			

Scoring

Add up your total number of yes answers in each section and record the scores below in the appropriate boxes. (Sometimes and no answers score no points.)

SECTION		TOTAL YES ANSWERS
Section One	EVA	_____
Section Two	KENDRA	_____
Section Three	NIXA	_____
Section Four	BELINDA	_____
Section Five	DIANA	_____
Section Six	ERIKA	_____

The section with the highest score is your #1 Guide. Write in the name that is next to your highest score:_____ .

The other five Guides are your Helping Guides. Rank them in order, starting with the highest number first and continuing until the lowest number.

Your Helping Guides are: _____
_____
_____
_____
_____
_____

3

Getting to Know Your Guides: Eva, Kendra, Nixa, Belinda, Diana, and Erika

In this chapter, you will be introduced to your feminine Guides. Each Guide has her own special attributes and qualities — and you will learn how to work with each of them to receive and accept Inner Feminine Power and actualize it to serve your own best interests in everyday life. The Guides will also be available to teach you their secrets and give you powerful messages that can be a source of strength when you need it most.

The Feminine Guides are inner partners that you rely on every day. They have their strengths and weaknesses, as you will see. Your #1 Guide (as determined by the Femininity Assessment Quiz) is the Guide that you identify most closely with. The other Guides, which we call Helping Guides, are the ones you call on less frequently — but which nevertheless can be enormously powerful in certain situations. All the Guides obey their true feminine nature . . . without repressing or denigrating their own uniqueness.

The six Guides, their signs, and main attributes are:

•   °   •

Getting to Know Your Guides

♡ **EVA**
the Enchantress: alluring, passionate

□ **KENDRA**
the Actualizer: goal setter, striver in the world

○ **NIXA**
the Free Spirit: creative, playful

◻ **BELINDA**
the Nurturer: provider, protector

☽ **DIANA**
the Independent: loner, loves solitude

△ **ERIKA**
the Wise Woman: intuitive, sees and discovers fate

The Guides represent the characteristics of feminine nature. They are not meant to be actual people, but are explained and described here so that you can easily recognize their attitudes and behavior patterns as your own. Getting to know the Guides will give you a better understanding of yourself and your relationships. During the course of getting acquainted with the Guides, you will also be getting in touch with the deep parts of your inner being.

Some of the elements you contact will seem familiar to you, others will be new. Self-knowledge is an important step in attaining Inner Feminine Power. Once you understand the forces that are influencing you, you will be energized toward positive self-change and growth. You will be able to *activate* your Inner Feminine Power to bring your whole life into the positive focus you always imagined was possible. In this chapter, you will learn how your Guides think, feel, and act. In the following chapters, you will learn how to use this knowledge to reclaim your full feminine powers.

Femininity is diverse . . . and complex. Just as you need to call upon many different parts of yourself in different experiences, you also want to be able to reach those parts of yourself when necessary—and, most importantly, you want to be able to *use* those parts of yourself fully and powerfully to effect meaningful change.

Curiously, the more complex and broad ranging you become, the simpler your whole life will be. When you can immediately reach within your myriad self for exactly what you want and need and use it for the right action, you know that powerful inner forces are at work. The more inner resources you have available to you, the more power you will have available.

Dominant forces within you affect growth and relationships. Why do some women choose men who are creative and successful, while others pick out men who are immature losers? Why are some women able to make the most of their careers and families, while others are constantly frantic and overwhelmed? Why are some women doubtful and fearful of the strength of their power? There are no simple answers to these questions—but the ability to know yourself in all aspects and to contact your Inner Feminine Power is the most important factor for self-change and growth in any situation or experience.

Just as your whole life fans out and becomes broader and richer, so your feminine self expands and opens more and more as different parts of it are acknowledged, contacted, and actualized by the force of your own Inner Feminine Power.

Let's begin by using the symbol of the fan to demonstrate the expanding and contracting nature of femininity. The image of the fan also represents the six Inner Guides and shows, in a graphic way, how they join together as one flexible and effective unit.

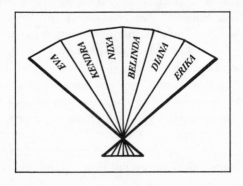

When the fan is completely open, all the Guides can be seen and contacted. Since they are all available to you, there is a sense of wholeness, harmony, and balance in your own femininity; all your inner resources are available, and their power is available too. This is called Inner Feminine Unity.

When the fan is completely closed, none of the Guides is available to you. When this happens you can feel at sea, rudderless, and in the dark about yourself, your relationships, and the direction you should take. Issues are murky; decisions, when made, are haphazard and arbitrary. You may feel depressed, out of touch, or angry. Sometimes, it can seem as if something's missing in your life, or that you just don't feel feminine.

For most of us, the fan is usually partway open, so that one or more of our Guides is influencing and helping our progress. At the present time, your #1 Guide is the one who is ruling your life or helping you the most. If she is taking over, you may need to call up a Helping Guide for balance ... and to help you to find the undeveloped, missing parts of yourself that remain hidden deep within. The function of the Helping Guides, then, is to enable you to open the fan completely and achieve Inner Feminine Unity. When you recognize and acknowledge what *all* the Guides can offer, you enlarge your boundaries and your power.

Your #1 Guide may change in different life phases. If Diana is now your #1 Guide, it means that at this particular time, Diana is most influential in helping you with self-change, relationships, and decisions in the sometimes mysterious process of being a woman.

On the following pages, you will get to know each of the Guides—Eva, Kendra, Nixa, Diana, Belinda, and Erika. Visualize each slat of the fan painted with a different design and color. Similarly, each of the Guides has different characteristics. In the course of opening and closing the fan, as in the course of a balanced life, harmony will prevail.

As you begin to understand the attitudes and patterns of the Inner Guides in the areas of love, work, money, friendships, and finding happiness, you'll start to recognize and acknowledge those same attributes in yourself.

In reading this material, remain open. Listen with your heart to the voices that speak to you. With watchfulness and mindfulness, begin in your own time. Remember when expanded to its fullest, the fan can cool passions or fan the flames of desire—and it can hide or reveal.

First read the attributes of your #1 Guide and continue with the other Helping Guides in the order that they appear in your Femininity Assessment Quiz. For example, if Kendra is your #1 Guide, and your Helping Guides are (in order) Diana, Eva, Belinda, Erika, and Nixa, read the text that follows in that order, flipping back and forth in the chapter to do so.

Your #1 Guide is your strongest, most authoritative Guide, and you call upon her more than any other. But different situations and relationships demand different approaches and a different kind of feminine courage, strength, and dignity. Instead of listening to stereotyped feminine ideals and role models, learn to listen to the *true* feminine voices inside yourself. What Kendra or Eva say to you will be unique to *your* experience, your feelings, and your deeply held beliefs.

In this chapter you will get to know your Guides in their positive and negative aspects. In the next chapter, "Putting Your Guides to Work," you will learn to empower them and channel that power to suit your best interests—whenever you want to.

Eva, the Enchantress

Eva celebrates her body and appreciates the joy and pleasure of lovemaking. She is *not* a man's conception of a sex goddess. For women, that precept is not empowering. Eva is attuned to her *own* need to be fascinating, glamorous, charming, and bewitching. She's a temptress because it's in her nature to be attuned to the interplay of love and life. Like Aphrodite, she invites her lover to enjoy her caresses and the tenderness of sex.

Eva's primary power is derived from her sensuality—and she emphasizes that quality rather than rationality and abstract thinking. In the sway of her hips, she reveals the intelligence of pleasure. Eva may very well be a femme fatale, a coquette who flirts outrageously and delights in seduction. This is Eva's knowledge and wisdom at work.

Eva attracts by entrancing. She entices by being naturally warm, seductive, open. Her eroticism embodies a taste for adventurous and exciting relationships. Eva is at times flooded with desire, and in this desire she seeks to please. Eva is also in charge of her pleasure and seduction—and, in this, she subtly induces others to please her. Eva controls what she will reveal and what she won't. In matters of fidelity, she can be evasive. She sometimes has little sense of propriety and doesn't feel obligated to "fess up."

Eva *is* beautiful, so she doesn't have to *make* herself beautiful, although she does use makeup, perfume, jewelry, and fashionable clothes to dress up her natural lustiness. But Eva realizes that her beauty has little to do with consumer products.

Eva is concerned with the art of giving herself, and it is in lovemaking that she becomes alive to her own femininity.

In her negative aspects, Eva's activities function as merely sexual release. When she becomes disconnected from her true feminine, frigidity or disgust may lead her away from sex altogether. Since Eva's raison d'être is grounded in the presence of a partner, this disconnectedness can lead to disruption, pain, and frustration. It is here that Eva needs to understand how her path to her feminine is blocked. What is at stake is communication with her own essential being. Eva can open doors with positive images instead of shutting doors with negative and self-limiting constraints.

Eva must continually keep in touch with her own nature and not become the reflection of a sex-obsessed society. Since she is filled with sexual wishes, she seduces to be set afire. Eva is a graceful siren, but in her negative aspects, she may become trivial, trite, and tawdry.

Eva embodies joy and pleasure. In her negative aspects, she embodies vanity and hedonism.

Eva finds her femininity in lovemaking. Orgasm leaves her with a feeling of strength, power, and fullness.

Friendships

Eva is invigorated by lovemaking, and in her friendships (nonsexual and sexual) that energy is present. Allure and charming ways are her enticements. She is always "on," and she has a knack for drawing attention to her sexual life force. She values it above everything and disperses it in the air like strong perfume.

She wants friends to admire her natural guile and assertive sexuality. The combination can be overwhelming because of its intensity. She can be competitive, jealous, and cunning, but she can also be a loyal friend—one who has deep, thought-out perceptions about love, which she is willing to share. Sexuality is her strength and lovemaking her nourishment. Eva will give a friend good counsel in *all* matters of the heart. You can go to her knowing that she will understand your love problems. Should I take the first step toward reconciliation? Is my heart really in lovemaking? What are my chances of getting closer sexually? Like a love oracle, Eva can help answer questions like these keeping her friend's best interests at heart.

But Eva gives more than advice. She conveys the power, the importance, and the binding force of sexual love. When that force is weakened or absent altogether in a friend's life, she shows how to attract or strengthen it. In this situation, Eva has no problems giving her secrets freely. As an advisor in love matters, she wants her guidance to be respected and appreciated.

Because of her appeal, Eva needs to be aware of jealousy in others. She exemplifies attractive and spontaneous sexuality, which is an idealized image of our times. That Eva can follow her true nature and at the same time find societal approval is reason enough for other women to despise her. Women whose true nature lies in other areas (some of them not sanctioned by society) are often confused and envious when they encounter Eva. Hostility toward her can be the result, so a keen awareness on Eva's part is necessary to counteract misunderstandings.

Work

Eva's work brings her pleasure. Generally, she chooses an occupation that is exciting and challenging, and one in which she can express her love of beauty. Eva wants to attract attention and be recognized for her ability to carry out her ideas in an organized and capable way. Variety is the spice of her work life for Eva, and she enjoys taking charge of complex projects and traveling. Eva likes to move around; she's not one to sit behind a desk or conform to a strict nine-to-five schedule. Eva does best in a job that allows her to have high visibility and to be in charge of work that is related to beauty—such as art or architecture, fashion, cosmetics, etc.

Evaluating and understanding her career comes easily to Eva. Besides being in a job that's connected to beautiful things, comfort and material satisfaction are also motivating factors in her work life. She is drawn to a job that is financially satisfying. Eva doesn't expect fast results. She is patient and persistent—and she is determined to accumulate a bit of wealth. Without indulging in excessive risk taking, Eva can be daring when it comes to finding just the right job. And she expects to be financially successful.

If she falls short in her first efforts, she will seek new opportunities for financial gain. Eva is spirited and self-assured, and she sees minor failures and disappointments as experiences that can lead to new growth. If for some reason, she fails to take right action, it is not a cause for self-recrimination or guilt. Rather, Eva looks upon the situation as a learning experience.

Eva's rewards come from having a job that is somehow connected to beauty and from material gain. A salary raise, a promotion, an upgrade in job title are all sources of satisfaction for her. Happiness in the workplace, for Eva, is not only linked to financial success, but she must be in an occupation that allows her to answer to her own inner needs. She needs on-the-job time and space to express her sense of beauty, and she needs to be respected for her efforts.

Money

Eva uses money to make the most of her natural attractiveness. Sometimes, just the right clothes or cosmetics or perfume are what she spends her money on. But most often she will use her money on such unglamorous things as maintaining good health, nutrition, and fitness. Her body is important to her, and she wants to keep it in shape. Whether she's involved in yoga or aerobics classes or sailing lessons, she views it as an activity that enhances her womanliness, not merely as a sport or exercise.

Discipline in money matters comes easily to Eva. A large part of her budget goes into pampering herself, and she will make sure that she has the extra time to sit in the sauna or steam room, or take that long, hot herbal bath. Eva can indulge herself in expensive chocolates or satin sheets because she builds some extravagances into her overall financial plan, making sure that bits of luxury are a part of her life. Discipline in Eva's case does not mean austerity, it means acting according to her rules.

Eva is often generous and gives gifts freely—and is gracious and accepting when she is on the receiving end. Sometimes materialistic, Eva, every now and then, looks at her possessions and questions their ability to nourish her inner self. She is also mindful not to link money and love together so that they constitute one reality.

About money, Eva's message is to freely use it for whatever contributes to strengthening and enriching the power of love—for herself, for her partner, and for their relationship. Each person's needs and expectations for love are different, but money can surround and protect love. It can cushion love from shock, and it can energize love by giving it the variety and flexibility it needs. The combination of money and love can be used creatively and in nonmanipulative ways. And Eva knows how to link them together so that fulfillment is achieved.

The men Eva gets involved with often have love/money confusions—equating or substituting one with the other in various ways. If she is being manipulated by her partner, Eva needs to create some emotional distance in order to sort out the specific instances and details. In this way, balance can be restored.

Love Relationships

In love relationships, Eva takes the sexual initiative. Playful and loving, she asserts her needs as a woman who is attuned to her own rhythms. She is never aggressive, but rather Eva strives for a sexual union that is satisfying to herself and her partner. This, for her, is the fulfillment of love. In lovemaking, she gives and receives caresses joyfully, and she can think up imaginative ways to heighten sensual pleasures.

Eva is not often disappointed in love. She is sincere in her own womanliness, and she expects—and usually finds—a partner who can give her the attention she wants. Eva forms a strong union that can endure setbacks. Because she is discriminating in selecting a lover, the relationship starts off on solid ground and continues to maintain inner stability as it grows. Eva does best in a partnership that allows her to express the full range of her sexuality. Her nature insists that nothing about love should be mechanical or contrived—and, for Eva, sex is the deepest expression of love.

Eva believes in complete honesty, and in relationships she requires integrity and strength of character. If there is a rift between her and her partner, she believes that closeness can be regained by directing awareness to true feelings and by confronting the underlying issues. Eva is adept at cutting through any romantic illusions or obstructions that impede progress. And her partner usually has the same attributes. Together they can reconcile their differences with candor and create new bonds that foster communion and connectedness rather than distance and separateness.

A humdrum life is not for Eva. She will go to great lengths to infuse variety and excitement into the relationship. Experiences that reward the senses—travel, eating fine food, listening to music—are highly valued. Enjoyment is the key word. Eva wants her relationships to *feel* luxurious. And in them things are seldom at a standstill; life moves forward in a way that is enriching and rewarding.

Eva is attracted to introverted, creative men. If he is moody and repressed, however, the relationship usually doesn't work well. Since Eva demands strong, emotional responses, she soon sees this type as a dud because he keeps his feelings buried. But if a man is intense, and if he has accumulated an emotional vocabulary, a strong bond can be created between them. Eva has no use for men who are eternal adolescents, undisciplined, or loners. She does best with stable, deeply erotic men who love her immeasurably without being possessive.

Finding Happiness

For Eva, happiness is to be found in love and sexual pleasures. She feels most complete in lovemaking. The sexual act and the love that accompanies it are transformative for Eva. She feels energized and charged by their power. In sexual union with a person she loves, she can share her innermost self.

Usually Eva does not have to seek love—it comes to her. Since she feels attuned to her true nature, she expects to attract a person who will give her the devoted, affectionate companionship she wants. Being able to find a suitable partner when she needs one gives her a feeling of increased self-esteem and self-confidence. Eva derives power from being connected to her sexual nature and to the love that surrounds it.

Eva enjoys being in the limelight. When the focus is on her, she basks in it contentedly. If her career is one in which she can take center stage—at meetings, on the telephone, or on business-related travel—she is pleased. She can blithely ignore those who don't pay attention to her, but Eva is never really rude or inconsiderate.

Eva can be a straight shooter, honest, and kind. Eva feels most comfortable with people who have integrity. Eva is lucky in love; she's seldom betrayed. But if that should happen, she recognizes it as a temporary setback and places her own needs first. Happiness in this instance comes from the experience of reevaluating and reorganizing her priorities in her own best interests. Being able to create this balance brings her joy.

Kenдra, the Actualizer

Kendra is a woman of the world. She's what you think of when you think about "today's woman"—a woman who wants it all. Kendra embodies the feminine qualities that are most admired in today's society. She shows herself (and the world) what it means to be courageous, powerful, steadfast, and persevering. Kendra challenges and inspires. Being very work oriented, she creates and strives and is always ready to fight for her own needs and rights. Kendra is well organized and can organize and stimulate those who work with her.

Time and scheduling are primary concerns—she understands the value of her time and expects to be well compensated financially.

She's a person who takes advantage of every opportunity and makes the most of it.

It's fairly easy for Kendra to live up to her convictions and strong motivations. And, if necessary, she will cut away old patterns and habits that have outlived their usefulness. She has a "female warrior" energy that enables her to destroy what is dead and extraneous.

Courage and dedication are her watchwords, and whether they're carried through in an idea or a way of being, she is always strong, self-confident and clear-eyed. Her intelligence resonates with accomplishment, and she often fights for human dignity.

Kendra uses logical and reasonable words to convey her intellectual foresight. Her internal mentor helps her combine objectivity and necessity, and she is ready for whatever comes her way.

In Kendra's negative aspect, she is addicted to perfection. She wants everything to be just so and under her control. Kendra finds it very difficult to relax and simply let things *be*.

Kendra may also have exceptionally high expectations for herself and others. She may demand or expect perfection in relationships—the "perfect" husband or the "perfect" child. She has to realize that *living* a relationship, or friendship, or motherhood is not just another project to be scheduled and undertaken. *Feelings*—hers and those of others—need to be addressed. There are times when objectivity cannot be substituted for feelings. And an opinion, instead of an emotional response, is inappropriate in certain situations.

Discernment, criticism, and judgment play a large part in Kendra's life, but they must give way, at times, to passion and joyousness.

Kendra's feminine power is derived from her spirit of action, not in the accomplishment itself (no matter how valuable). Her power resides in her ability to get the job done, without giving in to obstruction or constraint. Unlike Nixa, she is not fanciful or "inspired." She is systematic, and by sheer will and courage attains her goals. Personal feeling, pain, and pleasure are usually disregarded.

Friendships

Close friendships are important to Kendra. With women she needs the sisterly contact that best friends can provide. She loves to gossip and laugh, but she can be hesitant about sharing her feelings with even the closest friend. The intimate details of Kendra's emotional life are things she keeps to herself. She may not be able to express the joy of motherhood or the deep inner pain of losing a job promotion.

Helping a friend through a crisis or giving advice comes easily to Kendra. She is objective, loyal, and considerate. Most of all, she is reliable. You can always count on Kendra to be there. She can handle any situation with her friend's best interest in mind, but she tends to deal with problems in an action-oriented way, and when emotional issues are at stake, she's less helpful.

In friendships Kendra deals with logistics rather than emotional content. If a friend is having a problem with a teenage son, for example, Kendra concentrates on the steps to take rather than on her friend's feelings. If Kendra wants advice about a family problem of her own, she approaches it from an objective instead of a feeling point of view. On an objective level, Kendra is a clear thinker and can always be relied on to focus directly on the situation; on an emotional level, she often misreads friends' requests to explore the feelings involved.

What Kendra needs most from her friends is attention. She wants positive reenforcement that she is tops. Since Kendra likes to think of herself as the queen bee, friends often may be asked to support this self-image. Attention from friends is most rewarding for Kendra when it is focused on her accomplishments. She wants and expects her friends to appreciate her efforts. An extra pat on the back gives her a feeling of greater self-esteem.

Generosity is an important factor in Kendra's friendships. Gift giving is viewed as a reward for a friend's attention and loyalty. It is also a positive way of showing appreciation, a concrete measure of the value she places on the friendship. But she does this without thought of getting a gift in return. Tit-for-tat generosity is not for Kendra. Again, it is the queen bee mentality working here. Kendra bestows beneficence on those she can trust and count on. She gives to friends what she treasures most for herself—and that is "reward."

Kendra's style in friendship is to manage it. A dominant factor for her is to be in control. Appointments and commitments are allocated, sometimes ruthlessly, according to available time. Priorities are arranged quite systematically in Kendra's mind, with room for day-to-day contingencies.

Kendra's friendships with men are friendly and noncompetitive. She feels secure in her world and treats men as equals. She is at ease with men as nonsexual companions. Men seek Kendra's friendship because she's forthright and direct. However, to her, it's the dynamics of the friendship that matter, not gender.

In general Kendra tends to be judgmental in friendships. She has high standards and expects her friends to live up to her somewhat perfectionist attitudes. In this respect it is necessary for Kendra to develop her softer side so that compassionate attitudes can emerge.

Work

Work and a solid effort toward a goal are motivating factors for Kendra. Since she is well organized, it is easy for her to put together even the most complex projects. Whatever field she's in—science, the arts, business—she has the ability to see the overall picture and perform the task to its successful completion.

Both coworkers and professional supporters respond well to Kendra's enthusiasm and clear-headedness. She is looked upon by management as exceptional and promotable. Frequently she wins awards or attracts new business with her energy and self-confidence.

Kendra can manage her staff efficiently. Because her instructions and directions to them are clear and fair-minded, she usually gets the cooperation that is necessary for the workload. In hiring people she has a knack for spotting the right person, someone who will perform well. If her clothing store needs an assistant manager, for instance, she can immediately tell if the person she is interviewing has the necessary qualities to carry out the day-to-day responsibilities of running a retail business.

Achievement is high on Kendra's list of priorities. She wants to get ahead, and her vision of herself is of someone who usually succeeds at whatever she does. She wants to be paid well for her endeavors, and she has her eye on the next rung of the success ladder. But Kendra is the one that defines her own success. In professional situations she is not influenced primarily by external factors. Her inner drive is what motivates her.

If Kendra is married, has a family, or is in a love relationship with a man, those commitments are taken care of after her work commitments are satisfied. Whether she's a doctor, lawyer, or runs her own product-marketing company, achieving her own goals comes first and foremost.

In emergency work situations that require overtime, Kendra has no qualms about tackling the problems involved and solving them with calm unflappability. The people who work with her admire her strength and resolve. She remains considerate, polite, and to the point. After the emergency is over, she may be on the verge of collapse and need a few days of rest. But while the work-related crisis exists, her first priority is to get the job done.

Organizing time and money is easy for Kendra. If she is a management consultant, she can conceptualize and develop plans and then implement them. If she is an accountant, Kendra can easily direct her energies toward devising business plans or investment portfolios. Kendra is adept at finding a mentor who will, over a period of time, guide and support her career efforts.

On the logical side of things, Kendra is quite talented. In the emotional realm, however, she finds that she is cut off from her feelings because she doesn't let her emotions enter the workplace. When Kendra doesn't get the promotion she very much wants, or when she has to lay off coworkers because of company divestment, she doesn't let it get to her. She doesn't want to experience the full depth of her disappointment or concern. It is enough to think about it objectively and then go on to the next thing. Because she wants so much to maintain self-control, she loses touch with the heartfelt aspects of herself that she needs to fully develop in order to grow.

The rewards of work, for Kendra, are achieving her goals. It is her innate nature to organize and be responsible for the outcome. She will never be happy in a subordinate position, carrying out the concepts of others. A career that prevents her from taking charge will leave her depleted and mentally and physically fatigued. Frequent colds, allergies, and insomnia can result from a job that doesn't allow Kendra to build her own little empire.

Money

Money is never a major concern for Kendra. She is confident that money will rarely be a problem, and she believes that whatever she needs will be available for her. Kendra is naturally self-assured, and neurotic attachments to money are nonexistent. For her money is an accessible commodity to be used wisely. Being overly thrifty or a spendthrift is not a part of her nature.

Kendra gives freely. If, for example, it is necessary to pay her husband's law school tuition, she does it willingly. As a gesture of friendship she will offer a loan to an associate who is planning a trip on a tight travel budget. And she's quick to thank the people who help her. Subordinates at work, baby-sitters, nannies, housekeepers, mentors, etc. are all rewarded with small gifts of appreciation.

In Kendra's world, stability counts. Sound investments are important to her. Planning for a new home, children, a car, travel, retirement, etc. is easy for Kendra because it involves goals and achievement. Whether she's managing money by herself, with her partner, family, or an advisor, Kendra understands the extent of her financial needs—both on a long- and short-term basis.

For Kendra, money is a natural outgrowth of accomplishment. Success and money go together, and Kendra expects to be well paid for her professional work. When she isn't, she sets new sights for herself instead of sitting around feeling disappointed or sorry.

Kendra respects other people's idiosyncrasies about money. If her boyfriend undertips the waiter and splurges on an overpriced bottle of champagne all in the same evening, she accepts it as his nuttiness rather than judging his lack of common sense. She finds it just as easy to be with a friend who is downright stingy as with one who goes overboard with his credit cards.

In general, Kendra needs to be wary of others who want to tap her resources instead of using their own energies for financial gain. Hangers-on and no-goodniks who want to ride her coattails instead of hitching onto their own star need to be carefully pushed out of her life.

Love Relationships

Kendra chooses her partners carefully—and they're not necessarily successful, well-established men. Although she often looks for a handsome hero-type, her underlying need is for a lover who will let her move along unhindered in her career path and who will not be too sexually demanding. When Kendra makes a wise choice, the relationship will grow stronger through mutually rewarding experiences. A foolish choice can burden her with a partner who is uncaring and unfeeling or unfaithful.

In love relationships, Kendra tends to dominate her partner. She is aware of this and constantly tries to play down her controlling nature. One way she does so is by trying to let her heart rule instead of her head. But she is headstrong, she wants her way, and finds it difficult to give in to her emotions.

With her partners she is considerate, but at times finds it hard to be accommodating when decisions have to be made. Since Kendra is extremely capable and gets things done with ease and grace, she sometimes takes over without giving her partner a chance to have a say in the matter. Here, her own strategic thinking can be a saving grace. When Kendra focuses on her shortcomings, she usually sees that she doesn't always have to take the lead. Allowing her partner to share in shaping a relationship can strengthen the bonds of love.

Although Kendra does not have a strong sexual nature, she can enjoy love play when she gets in touch with her body and the way it responds to affectionate caresses. To do this, Kendra needs to put aside the controlling aspect of her nature. With a lowkey but sexually interesting partner, she can learn to let go. The more Kendra allows herself to unwind and relax, the more she will be able to participate in her own and her partner's sexual fulfillment.

Surprisingly, Kendra does appreciate romance. When her lover remembers her birthday with an antique ring or takes her to a new restaurant, she is deeply pleased. Good manners and old-fashioned thoughtfulness are important to her.

Discussions about emotions and feelings between Kendra and her man are infrequent. The logistics of coming and going take precedence—what work was like today, what movie to see on Friday, where to go on vacation, who to see this weekend.

Kendra and her partner are usually faithful companions. Their love relationship is stable, but if it gets rocky because of her partner's infidelity (it's not in Kendra's nature to have an affair), they talk it out or go to a counselor to resolve the conflict. Kendra wants to be numero uno, and she has a great difficulty even thinking about another woman lurking in the background. To her, unfaithfulness indicates a great lack of character.

Kendra is attracted to a man who's a winner; losers turn, her off. In the latter category, Kendra lumps together men who are perpetual adolescents, men who can't act decisively, men who want a free lunch, and men who look to her for permission to start their life. She is attracted to a man who is fully capable of seeing her as a self-actualizing person, a man who can appreciate her strength and forcefulness without leaning on her.

In general, love relationships are mutually satisfying for Kendra and her partner. They are usually on solid ground and based on the interests and concerns of two people who are in agreement on how they want to live their lives. Neither one is overly dependent on the other. If Kendra's partner sometimes becomes immature or irrational, she has no problem guiding him to healthier attitudes by using gentle persuasion. Kendra uses objectivity instead of emotional wiles to present her case effectively.

Finding Happiness

Kendra is happiest when she is accomplishing something—whether it's at work, on the tennis court, traveling, wherever. Domesticity doesn't interest her because the routine seems to clog up her gears. Kendra's nature is an actualizing one, and she is at her best when she is involved in a project that she can direct. In ancient times,

Kendra would probably have been Queen of the Nile—enlisting armies and directing pyramids and temples to be built.

Work to Kendra is stimulating and energizing. It is the way she uses herself to her own best advantage. Whether Kendra is a researcher, lawyer, or an administrative assistant, she feels enriched by her profession.

In this context, Kendra needs a stable environment in which to function. Home and workplace should be in harmonious balance so that the home supports the work effort. Family, marriage, and love relationships should all support Kendra's primary satisfaction—work. Once these priorities are recognized, love and relationships can have their own secure places in Kendra's life. Acknowledging the importance of work need not override and overshadow other family or friendship considerations. Nor does it denigrate or relegate them to oblivion. It merely recognizes that work brings the greatest happiness to Kendra because it satisfies her ambition.

Since Kendra lives purposefully and deliberately, she is often cut off from deep feelings—her own and others'. This can make her development a little lopsided and keep her from experiencing the kind of happiness that emotional intensity and passion can bring into her life. To find genuine happiness, it is necessary for Kendra to allow herself to live on a more feeling and instinctual level at times. To go beyond her own sometimes armored perceptions, Kendra needs to begin to empathize with the feelings of her lover, friends, and children. Also, when Kendra allows her head to rule and keeps an emotional distance from her sexuality, her relationship or marriage can dwindle down to simple companionship or convenience.

For Kendra, finding happiness is an achievable goal. Once she makes the effort to cultivate her underdeveloped emotional range, she's on her way.

Nixa, the Free Spirit

Nixa is impatient with the status quo. She likes change and whatever is "new." She has the capacity to challenge the old order of things with her intelligence and charm. Playfulness and a childlike quality enliven and animate her personality.

Nixa has faith in her creativity. Imagination and a heartfelt vision of life are her paramount qualities. She is airy and light—and her spirit shines in her eyes. Nixa is almost always enthusiastic and spontaneous.

Wisdom, for Nixa, is the ability to cut through established concepts and bring forth new images of the way things could be. She "plays" with her thoughts, and many times, in what others would call frivolous, idle contemplation, she finds new patterns and makes new connections. In work she gives highest expression to her curiosity. Nixa expects that what she doesn't yet know will prove to be interesting.

Nixa is open-minded and willing to consider new ideas, concepts, and feelings—even though she may have to change her own opinions or decisions. And, in her open-mindedness, she is adaptable. Since she's never locked into existing arrangements, she is always free to try new plans to meet new situations.

Nixa loves life, and she has a zest for experience. She is flexible and tolerant in her live-and-let live attitude. Nixa rarely passes judgment on the actions of other people—she would rather try to understand their viewpoint.

Decision making for Nixa is impulsive and spontaneous. It is not the result of planning. In fact, Nixa is accomplished at handling the unplanned and unexpected.

On the negative side, Nixa has a tendency to fly high. She doesn't want to miss anything. She takes great pleasure in starting something new, but when the newness wears off, she often doesn't sustain the effort necessary to see the project through. In her negative aspect she can be the Hare in "The Tortoise and the Hare," operating in spurts of brilliance but lacking judgment.

Balance is necessary here, and Nixa must learn to take pleasure in finishing what she begins.

Making effective life choices requires, at times, for Nixa to be more grounded in perceptive discipline.

Nixa derives her feminine powers from an ability to be ready for anything and everything. Her unbound curiosity

and imagination enliven and fuel her spirit, and she lives life
to its creative hilt.

Friendships

Nixa has many friends, and she finds it easy to make new friends
wherever she goes. She picks friends who are imaginative and
quick witted. Spontaneity is an important characteristic in her
friendships—she picks up and goes off somewhere at the drop of a
hat, and she expects her friends to be ready. Nixa loves being
surprised, whether it's an elaborate party or a poem from a friend.
She also likes to surprise her friends with gifts, even if it's for no
special occasion other than as a token of friendship. She is
enthusiastic about her friendships and tries to be creative about
expressing her feelings. Her gifts are sometimes unusual—a jar of
small colored stones from a trip to Nepal, an assortment of postage
stamps in a homemade paper folder, a pencil drawing—but they
are always given joyfully to celebrate the friendship.

Since Nixa has many interests, she chooses friends who she can
talk to about a variety of subjects. Nixa also has a wide emotional
range, and she wants to be able to express her extremes of
happiness, sorrow, anger, frustration, disappointment, etc. If she is
involved in the arts, Nixa wants her friends to understand her
feelings toward work-related problems.

Nixa feels close to her friends, and she thinks of them as a
support group she can count on to be emotionally available. The
stress and strain of everyday life are easier for Nixa to cope with
when she feels that her friends are there for her. Nixa is empathic,
and she will listen intently and compassionately to a friend's travails
and triumphs. Whether it's a discussion about adopting a child or
the joy of winning first prize in a crafts contest, Nixa puts her heart
into the friend's situation.

What Nixa looks for most in friendships is a sense of community.
Each friend, as she sees it, is part of a whole network she can count
on when necessary. If she needs help writing a term paper or wants
to talk about marriage plans, she is reassured to find an understand-

ing ear and get helpful information. Nixa feels that she is part of this community of friends, and she's very willing to give as much support as she receives.

Nixa loves people. She seeks out friends that she feels are interesting, and she is creative when it comes to friendships that are getting bogged down. She wants her relationships with others to be stimulating, intellectually and emotionally, and when a friendship gets dull, she finds ways to revive it. Sometimes it is a question of doing something new and different together; other times the friendship may need some quiet time to talk about feelings. Or what may be needed is a pause in the friendship—a period of time away from each other to grow separately and then later come together to reclaim the friendship in a new way.

Nixa is never content with the status quo, and she is always on the lookout for ways friendships can grow and prosper. She is sensitive to the give-and-take in her friendships and is usually open-minded, aware of her friends' needs, and able to give heartfelt responses. Nixa knows how friendships can deepen, and she also recognizes how her own personal growth affects the friendship.

In general, Nixa infuses her friendships with her own special brand of creativity and panache. She has spontaneity and style, and she uses them to liven things up.

Work

Nixa enjoys work that is creative—and would be happy as an artist, hair stylist, chef, photographer, urban planner, etc. She wants to be able to use her imagination in a way that is rewarding. At times she has good business sense, but she prefers to devote her talents to developing her ideas and concepts. If possible, an assistant is at hand to help her with logistics, details, and follow-through.

Long hours of work are not uncommon for Nixa. Once she gets going, her concentration doesn't fade. She feels most alert and alive when she is following her inspiration. The finished product, to Nixa, is not as important as the act of creation. If she is a weaver, the excitement of spinning and dyeing the wool and creating the pattern of cloth is more interesting to her than the finished blanket.

Nixa is dedicated to her work. She is very aware that her creative energies must be actualized—and that her personal growth and satisfaction are derived from being involved firsthand in the creative process. Her zeal is almost limitless, and she sometimes goes overboard in immersing herself in her work. She feels rewarded and enriched by it. Work is play, and play is work; for Nixa, there is no difference.

If Nixa finds herself in a job situation that is routine, or one in which she has to compromise, she can become bored, lethargic, or depressed. If she feels that she is unable to use her imagination fully, she can become restless and have headaches, insomnia, or other physical symptoms. Any stifling of her natural talents can produce diminished energy and a disinterested attitude.

But Nixa is a smart cookie. She can usually get herself back into gear. Nixa is dependent on being fulfilled creatively, and she will go to great lengths to satisfy her needs.

Money

Nixa is care*free* about money, but not necessarily care*less*. She has no problem spending money on herself. If she is buying clothes, she will select just the right outfit—one that she feels will bring out her best features. Instead of looking for sale items, she looks for the clothes that feel perfect. She prefers to have a few good-looking clothes rather than a lot of items purchased because they were good buys. Clothes are important to Nixa, and she often picks out combinations that suit her individualistic attitudes.

If Nixa has money to spare, she will spend it freely on friends, restaurant dinners, concerts, travel, etc. She has no problem with financially supporting a partner, if necessary. Nixa has few emotional ties to money. She is fairly objective and has a vague budget, but she doesn't always know or care how the money gets spent.

Creativity is her gold mine of possibilities, and Nixa is very aware of the part money plays in her creative life. She needs it for things like art supplies, a computer, or clerical help.

Nixa usually doesn't pay much attention to investments or

savings. If she has an available chunk of money, she would rather put it into renting a beach house for the summer or buying a trendy-looking car. Accumulating money in long-term securities doesn't interest her. She would rather use it in a way that brings instant gratification and pleasure.

Financial independence is absolutely necessary for Nixa. She wants to be in complete control of her own money. Whether she's a teenager or in advanced old age, her security is linked to a large amount of available money. Since Nixa is very often impulsive, the misuse of credit cards can sometimes be a problem. She is generous and giving and may have to be careful about overextending herself.

Love Relationships

Nixa sees herself as a live wire, but when it comes to love relationships her luck sometimes seems to fizzle. She is attracted to partners who aren't quite as emotionally perceptive as she would like. What Nixa wants from her partner is someone who understands and picks up on her many moods. She wants her partner to relate to the ups and downs of her life and give her day-by-day encouragement, and to support her creative efforts.

Nixa can fall in love intensely. She throws herself wholeheartedly into her relationships and expects them to deepen and grow. With an affectionate partner, sex is varied and imaginative. She enjoys prolonged lovemaking, often with a younger partner. Nixa considers herself sexually alive and is willing to tell her lover what pleases her and what doesn't. She wants a monogamous relationship, but not necessarily one that involves a deep commitment or marriage. Responsibility and working things out are not things that enter into Nixa's thinking.

Creativity rules all aspects of Nixa's life, and love relationships are no exception. She expects that she and her partner will be imaginative in all that they share—whether that's lovemaking, cooking, household maintenance, sports activities, or just plain hanging out. Nixa has a carefree attitude, and careful planning is not part of her repertoire. If the morning is sunny and cool, she and her partner may spontaneously decide to take a picnic lunch to the waterfall or take the kitchen chairs into the backyard and refinish them.

Nixa's attitude can be joyous, and is, in part, fueled by being in love. When things are going well between her and her partner, she feels renewed and invigorated. Her own creative endeavors go more smoothly, and her chores get done easily. Nixa is most always in touch with the depths of her creative nature, and she is most at home in an open, flowing relationship. True union, for Nixa, is a feeling of uniting with a partner while at the same time retaining her separate self.

When Nixa gets involved in a love relationship that does not allow room for this separate self to flourish, she feels angry and disappointed. If her partner is overly demanding, jealous, or possessive, Nixa feels her creative powers diminishing. The time and effort needed to make things right, and the emotions expended, are de-energizing. She can become conflicted—wanting to leave the relationship and at the same time wanting to muster her forces to try to achieve the balance within the relationship that she needs.

In general Nixa's love life is ardent. She has a good idea about the kind of partner that will bring her satisfaction. But often, because of her fly-by-night attitudes about romance, she will get carried away by external characteristics such as attractiveness, wealth, or status. Nixa is aware that most of all she needs love and respect for her creativity. She needs acknowledgment from her partner that in the union between the two of them, there are also two separate selves to be attended to.

Finding Happiness

For Nixa, happiness and being creative are two sides of the same coin. Being able to use her imagination is the strongest motivating force in her life. She will persevere against all odds to ensure her creativity is allowed to be expressed. When negative things happen to her—disappointing love relationships, a missed career opportunity, family problems—she can maintain a harmonious balance as long as she is in touch with her deeply creative self.

Accomplishing this may be as simple as working out her psychic growth by keeping a dream journal. Or her artistic nature may lead her to writing poetry or painting watercolors. Nixa may want to work with fabric, embroidery, designs, quilting, or knitting. She may be interested in carpentry or landscape design. Whether it's a vocation or an avocation, staying in touch with her own creative process is what rules Nixa. It is her raison d'être and alters her whole being.

Nixa is very conscious of the rhythm of her life. From childhood on, she has always had a deeply rooted feeling about the beat of life—she knows how sometimes the pace is slowed down and at other times it's quickened. And she is aware of her own need to create a balance between the two modes. Listening to music—taped or live—often brings Nixa a great sense of peace.

Happiness in love relationships can be achieved if she finds a partner who appreciates and values her for herself. Creativity comes first. When Duke Ellington said, "Music is my mistress," he had the same idea. A love relationship for Nixa is important, but her creativity is primary.

Nixa gets along best with a partner who is an intellectual and emotional equal, one who is mature enough to give her the time and space for creative pursuits. If they both work on projects together, that also can bring Nixa fulfillment. For example, she and her mate could be a writer-artist team or partners in a catering business.

For Nixa, happiness is an everyday event. She welcomes change of her own making and is constantly reaching into her deep inner wellspring of creativity for new possibilities. Her potential for happiness is enormous, but it is always based on her own creative process.

Belinda, the Nurturer

Belinda is basically a homebody, but she's definitely not the stereotyped homemaker. She is responsible and wants commitment from her family and friends. Her life-giving, protective, and motherly qualities are obvious in her demeanor. Her very presence says "Mother Earth."

Belinda likes routine and schedule. She likes "nesting" and beautifying her environment. A congenial atmosphere is apparent in her living space, and she has the capacity to structure and order her home in ways that are welcoming to everyone who enters it. Her femininity receives and reassures—away from the tumult of the world.

She creates and maintains space so that all those who cross the threshold are refreshed. Cooking and the presentation of food are important to her. And the beauty of her surroundings often undergoes frequent change—she's always painting cupboards, sewing curtains, rearranging furniture.

Her empathy makes her very aware of other people's needs. She responds with motherly feelings and tactfulness. Most of the time she finds it easy to be practical and concrete. Advice, as such, is not given, but she guides and heals so that it seems what has been received is the milk of human kindness.

If Belinda has children, she gives them plenty of love but has fears and doubts about being a good mother. She has old-fashioned maternal values, but it is not necessary for Belinda to be a biological mother in order to express her motherly attributes. Belinda's maternal love (as it is given to herself, as well as to others) is the love of gestation and expectation. It is the love of being patient with ourselves and others. She understands that progress will happen anyway, whether we do anything about it or not.

In her negative aspects, Belinda can allow herself to become drained by people who want constant, unconditional love from her. Or she may become drained by maintaining friendships that demand she surrender mothering herself. It is only in caring in a tender, supportive way for our Inner Feminine that we can begin to care for others.

Maternal qualities are tender, supportive, and comforting, but they must be paired with discipline so that they don't become negative and lose their formidable power.

Belinda derives her feminine power from nourishing, listening, caring, and promoting growth. At her most feminine she provides primal warmth and the milk of human kindness.

Friendships

Belinda's friendships revolve around hearth and home. She has created her own living space in a way that invites mutual understanding between people. While Belinda is far from being the Good Mother of myth and fairy tale, her presence does exude a certain calm and serenity. Not the peacefulness of a Madonna, but rather the centeredness of a good friend who always has your best interests at heart.

Friendships with other women may take on a mother/daughter aspect, where the "daughter" looks to Belinda for guidance. The same thing may happen in friendships with men, where a mother/son aspect brings the man to seek out Belinda's warm maternal qualities and to rely on her motherly nature for reassurance.

Belinda's friendships are emotional in character. She thinks of herself as a mother hen keeping her chicks free of harm. She is protective and reassuring, while at the same time teaching fierce independence. When a friend is being eased out of her job by the company manager, Belinda has all the heartfelt words she needs to offer support and self-confidence. If a female friend is upset about having minor surgery, Belinda's there with positive affirmations and practical information.

Belinda connects with the deep inner needs of her friend. With her own centeredness rooted in the maternal process, she touches all those with whom she comes in contact with a positive force that can only be described as nourishing. Belinda nourishes the friend's spirit that needs to be mothered (and every person needs that every now and then).

Generosity, for Belinda, is meted out with thought and concern. Her door is always open and her cupboards are full and ready. Cooking is important to Belinda, but she's not the "chicken soup" type. Rather, she offers lovingly prepared and presented dishes. Sharing a meal is a way to celebrate a friendship. The table, for Belinda, is the measure of a person.

The most important thing Belinda expects in a friendship is appreciation. She wants her friends to value what she has to offer. And she wants them to express their feelings to her. Wholehearted giving is a standard by which Belinda lives, and she expects her friends to reciprocate by admiring her ability to give so lovingly. When a friend says, "This means a lot to me," Belinda gets the satisfaction she needs.

For Belinda, holidays, celebrations, and other rituals offer a way that friendships can grow and take on new meaning. During those times, she can create a sense of peaceful order in an atmosphere of warmth. Her most rewarding moments come when she can invite people to participate with her in activities that are meaningful and significant.

Belinda is like Mother Earth—she wants the world to grow green and blossom. In friendships, she needs to be wary of people who take advantage of her generous nature. Her power to be tender, supportive, and comforting can be drained by friends who need constant help. Discipline is very necessary here, and Belinda has to learn to say no. Although she may value the friendship, she cannot allow herself to be imposed on without setting limits. Courage and determination are especially needed here to balance her goodheartedness with her innocence and gullibility.

Work

Belinda finds it difficult to balance her professional life and the domesticity that she loves. Finding time to be with her family and attend to the needs of a home she cares about is not easy. When all the details of maintaining a home have to be compressed into an inadequate time frame, they become chores instead of age-old life-giving rituals.

Unless she can schedule her own work time, Belinda sees her job as something that keeps her away from the cycles of her life: nature, the seasons, the garden, her animals. Work is seen as a distraction that takes her away from what is "real." Instead of working as a real estate broker, she'd rather be at home making a quilt or putting up pints of strawberry jam. Belinda works to make money—to support herself, for school tuition, for a new roof. She has no elaborate career plans and no long-term work-oriented goals. Work, no matter how stimulating or high paying, takes her away from the things she loves most.

Work, for Belinda, is not all that it's cracked up to be. And, while she is organized and productive on the job, her heart is elsewhere. In positions such as teacher, social worker, nurse, hospice worker, etc., Belinda can use her nurturing qualities to best advantage and be emotionally rewarded as well. But in general, Belinda feels best when tending to the fires of her own home.

Belinda is capable on the job. As a manager, she is well liked by both her subordinates and her superiors. In getting the job done, however, Belinda sometimes feels that she has to suppress her valuable motherly qualities. By constantly being objective and devoting her attention to job objectives, she feels a loss of self-esteem.

If Belinda is a young mother, she is relieved and happy to spend a maternity leave with her baby. Away from the rhythm of the office, she can immerse herself in the mother/child cycle of nourishment and growth. The simple, elemental tasks of motherhood are rewarding and satisfying for Belinda.

Since Belinda is a homebody, going out to work is always difficult. She is happiest if she can schedule her time and also her work at home. Computer-related work, proofreading, editing or indexing, writing, or an at-home business could allow her the leisurely feeling she needs to thrive.

Belinda will succeed best in an occupation where she can guide and counsel others, and if she can be self-employed, so much the better. Because of her innate fair-mindedness, Belinda enjoys a job that allows her to look at both sides of a situation in a compassionate way—such as a marriage counselor, career counselor, teacher for the learning disabled, nutritionist, etc.

In general, Belinda's task is to create harmony between her true home-and-hearth nature and the workaday world that values power and strategy.

Money

Belinda is careful with money—not exactly thrifty, but she does compare prices at the food market, and buy clothes on sale. She spends her money on home-related items and is generous in seeing that her family's needs are met.

Travel isn't frequently in her budget. She'd rather use the money on things to make her home life more comfortable—a VCR, a pool table, a free-standing fireplace. Again, her selections are carefully researched for prices before she makes her purchases.

Belinda's emotional concerns about money are tied to her strong needs for a stable home life. Money, for Belinda, represents security. She wants to be sure that it is always available, and thus in leaner times Belinda is faced with emotional uncertainty. Since her stability depends on keeping hearth and home together, when her finances are shaky, she sees lack of money as a threat to her ability to create a nurturing home.

Belinda pictures herself as a generous, giving person, one who can provide whatever is needed. With enough money on hand, she can extend herself in ways that enrich her life and those of the people around her. When money is scarce, her self-image and self-confidence both suffer. Belinda enjoys being generous, whether it's sending the latest best-seller to her mother or bringing a bouquet of roses to a coworker who has AIDS.

Money is an emotional issue in Belinda's life. She is concerned that she might, for some reason, not have enough resources for everything she wants to do for herself, her family, and her friends. At times there is a tendency on her part to think of her partner as the provider rather than an equal participant in household financial affairs.

Investments, bank accounts, and securities are of great interest to Belinda. She is a saver and feels reassured by the knowledge that a nest egg is growing for the future. She's also hesitant about taking out loans and prefers to pay cash, if possible, even for large purchases, such as a car.

In general, Belinda's finances are tidy. She keeps a close watch over the money flow, and she has a good understanding of where the money goes.

When Belinda relies entirely on her lover or husband for economic support, she needs to assure herself of the value of her contribution to the household. The quiet serenity she creates in the home and the competitive pace of the workaday world should be complementary. Belinda provides a quiet inner way of being and her love provides her mate with an outer way of asserting himself in the world. In this traditional arrangement, it is necessary for Belinda to speak up when she feels that what she provides is discounted, devalued, or forgotten.

Love Relationships

Belinda falls in love forever. She commits herself fully to her partner and feels responsible for defining the relationship and for keeping it afloat when it gets into rough waters. Belinda is not controlling or competitive with her partner. She is caring and affectionate, attentive and attuned to the emotional needs of both her partner and herself.

What Belinda wants in love relationships is to rely on her partner's strength to be there for her when necessary. She needs the love and comfort that an intimate relationship can provide. Sharing ordinary day-to-day events gives Belinda a sense of continuity. The ordinariness of sitting down to dinner together, taking a hike in the woods, or replanting the herb garden all give Belinda a sense that she is connected to a cycle that is repetitive and abundantly pleasurable.

Sex is not of the utmost importance to Belinda. She is very aware of her own monthly cycle, and her sexual needs ebb and flow accordingly. She and her partner can usually find a mutually satisfactory pattern of lovemaking which will continue to please both of them through the years. Sex, for Belinda, is a low-key experience. She is ambivalent about the sexual act itself, and strong sexual urges or releases are not common.

What Belinda needs most is affection. She wants to be held and hugged and cuddled. She enjoys sex when it happens because it gives her the opportunity to communicate and express her maternal, caring self—and to get all the tenderness she needs. When sex isn't available, however, she doesn't miss it that much.

Belinda attracts men who aren't interested in being with a woman who has strong sexual desires, which usually suits her just fine. What she has to watch out for is a loss of sexual identity. By being ever watchful and mindful of her own sexual responses and her lover's, a separate sexual self can evolve over time. Otherwise, confusion and misunderstanding may result. Belinda must relate to her own sexuality, not have it defined by others.

Belinda prefers a monogamous relationship, and she chooses a partner whose attitude is similar. Going outside the home or marriage to seek out a lover is not something she can easily accommodate into her life. It goes against her grain to betray the person she loves.

The forever love Belinda wants so much to maintain fills her emotional need for steadiness. She sees herself and her partner as a couple bonded to each other by love and mutual respect, and by agreement they will cherish each other "until death do us part." The home and family is their common ground, and Belinda wants to create a life with her partner in which the relationship can thrive.

Finding Happiness

Belinda finds happiness in simple places. An ordinary day can be filled with many special moments—the smell of brewing coffee, a cardinal on the bird feeder, folding bed sheets after they have been drying in the sun. All these things give Belinda a sense of peace and contentment, and the routine of daily life gives her a feeling of wholeness. Inner peace, for Belinda, comes from doing things in their own time instead of trying to beat the clock. In a meditative way, she performs tasks and focuses on what she is doing rather than rushing through them.

The fulfillment of having a life partner and a family allow Belinda to feel completed. She is concerned with the home, but if she goes overboard, she may find herself overprotected and starry-eyed instead of being in touch with reality. As Bachelard said, "The house shatters day dreaming, the house protects the dreamer, the house allows one to dream in peace." Belinda has to set limits on just how much dreaming she wants to do.

Happiness for Belinda is not a goal to be sought after. Rather it is the accumulation of small things, year after year, that brings joy. Assembling photographs in an album, keeping a diary, serving on the town library committee—these all bring Belinda a feeling of self-worth and commitment. Taking on responsibilities that contribute to society—whether that's in the professional or volunteer area—will broaden her scope and encourage her to make new friendships.

Reading, gardening, crafts (such as quilting, needlepoint, woodworking, sewing), and cooking will allow Belinda to stretch her imagination. Caring for animals or plants can also bring feelings of increased self-esteem.

In general, finding happiness is not a route to be taken or a journey out into the unknown. In Belinda's life it is achieved through the quiet contemplation of the positive things that are available to her every day—and seeing how they add up through the years. Being in harmony with the cycles of nature (the seasons, the moon, the weather) brings the greatest joy.

Diana, the Independent

Diana finds her femininity in being alone. She is a woman who is one in herself—she belongs to herself, and her commitment is to her inner being. She is answerable only to herself. She is self-contained and, like Erika, men do not influence her. Neither one is dependent on men's approval.

Diana's involvement with men is mostly nonsexual. She has many men friends who understand her need for time alone—time to refine and explore her experience in the world, to sift and integrate what's happening, and to make future plans.

She is grounded and connected to things that have to be done *alone,* and she chooses friends who support this.

Diana is self-sufficient and uncompromising. She knows that by being alone she can reach the deep, inner wellsprings of her femininity. And she knows that the almost daily pattern of reaching and celebrating those unique moments is what enriches and nurtures her. She realizes that only by a steadfast loyalty to her inclination for solitude can she remain richly alive. Being in solitude informs the rest of her life of its deep meaning. It brings insights of who she is and who she might become.

Diana's femininity is found in solitude, where the cycles and patterns of her life can be felt and innately understood for what they are. Being alone is an absolute necessity, not a luxury, for Diana. It is only in her *chosen* solitude that she can return to a natural and primitive inner space where she sifts and sorts and integrates life. This solitary place of retreat empowers her. It is a place away from the patriarchal world of dominance and submission, a place where the art of exploring her femininity is honored. It is a place away from others and a time to recharge so that she can go back to work and relationships refreshed.

Diana, in her negative aspect, can easily become a hermit. Her overriding need to be alone can prevent emotional relatedness, and in relationships, it can certainly be a detriment. Because a life of solitude is so gratifying to Diana, it can turn into a form of escapism. Diana's task is to seek solitude *temporarily*, and to moderate her distance and separateness from the everyday world.

Balance is necessary—and it is also necessary for Diana to know how to go forward into solitude so that a strong connection to friends, a partner, or children is maintained.

Diana derives her feminine power from connecting to an "unspoiled" self. In solitude she can inform her life of its meaning, and later, bring that meaning into her world.

Friendships

Diana chooses friends who will give her the time and space to be herself when she needs to. She does not feel especially committed to her friends—Diana has a loose arrangement in friendships that allows her to come and go as she pleases. When she wants to spend time with a friend, she will. Otherwise, she won't. Because it is necessary for Diana to be alone a great deal, she schedules her time according to her deeper needs, not according to what is culturally approved.

Getting to Know Your Guides

Although Diana may have close women friends, she does not rely on them for support or approval. What she needs in a friend is companionship, someone to talk to, a person who will listen to her triumphs and trials. She wants someone to acknowledge her feelings, and she genuinely wants feedback. Most of all, she wants a friend to understand how and why she needs solitude.

Diana is able to be empathic. She can listen to a friend and understand; whether it's a friend's anger at a boyfriend or fear of taking a new job, she can commiserate. But if the friendship takes too much time away from her solitary pursuits, she can become resentful.

Diana can easily discard friendships when they are not going along as smoothly as she thinks they should. She is judgmental rather than accepting, and she has disdain and sometimes contempt for friends who don't meet her standards of behavior. She sets her own rules and is clear-cut in what she will tolerate and what she won't. Honesty and straightforwardness are traits that she admires in friends. They mean more to her than reliability. If a friend is late for an appointment three times in a row, it doesn't phase her. But if the same friend lies to her about the price of a painting she bought, Diana gets upset because the friend, in her mind, doesn't have "character."

Diana acknowledges that she needs to come out of her isolation once in a while, and she does enjoy the stimulation and camaraderie of friendship. Eating dinner in a restaurant, going to the movies, swimming, biking, and tennis are all activities that she enjoys with friends.

Diana doesn't like to complicate her life with friendships that are draining. She has little time or energy for people who have negative attitudes or who are self-destructive. Friends who are accepting and tolerant put her at ease.

What Diana wants most in a friendship is a feeling of communion. She likes the kind of genuine interchange where deep feelings can be expressed. This amicable sharing is a way that her deep convictions can be made known and can become valued by herself and her friends.

Friendships are important to Diana, and she likes to be with people who appreciate her spirited independence. Diana is quietly involved in pursuing her interests by herself—not selfishly or neurotically self-absorbed. Being alone is her nature, and friends are attracted to her for this reason. In friendships with men she is candid and noncompetitive. She is also understanding and considerate, but she won't go out of her way if the situation impinges on her time to be alone.

Work

Diana is most productive when she is working alone. Such careers as lab technician, statistician, computer programmer, or accountant offer a structure that will be rewarding. Diana enjoys her job and derives pleasure from performing well.

At work, as in other areas, her independent nature takes over. Socializing with coworkers, office gossip, and team efforts don't interest her. Diana wants to make a go of her career, but on her own terms. She is strong willed and doesn't take criticism well, even if it is constructive. Determination is a strong characteristic of hers, and she will persist at a task until she has completed it to her own satisfaction.

Diana is not especially sensitive to the feelings of her coworkers, and she can be outspoken or strident in her remarks. If she is in a managerial position, she expects her staff to perform well with a minimum of supervision. If she is a freelance artist or writer, she usually needs little guidance to complete the assignment.

Emotions don't play a big part in her work effort, and she is able to separate herself from the personalities of those she interacts with on the job. Office functions and office politics are things she tries to stay away from as much as possible. Diana sometimes feels like an outsider, but she has no desire to take part in activities other than her actual work.

Diana's feelings about her career are positive. She takes pride in her accomplishments, and she feels dedicated to supporting herself as luxuriously as she can. She sees work as something that brings stability into her life, and she appreciates the routine of it for that reason.

Getting to Know Your Guides

Money

Diana is easygoing about money and uses it to further her interests, such as travel, books, and computer software. She relies completely on herself to provide financial security. A stable job situation and savings are important to her. If Diana has a family, she is fair-minded about budgeting and allocating money where and when it is needed. Diana is practical and sensible, but occasionally she can be an impulsive shopper. It is not out of character for her to buy three sweaters in the same style but different colors or a down jacket she doesn't really need.

Money does not have the emotional grip on Diana that it does on most people. If it is available, she will spend it contentedly and wisely on what she considers just the right things. When money is tight, Diana can easily make do for a while. Having money or not having money does not affect her moods or feelings about herself. Her self-confidence and self-esteem are not tied in to cash flow. If she finds herself short of money, Diana does not become angry or panicky. Her response is a practical one, rather than an emotional one.

She does not use money as a means to control people. Withholding money or being generous are, for Diana, practical considerations, not methods to manipulate other people's emotions. Diana understands, however, that money *does* free her, to a certain extent, from dependence, and it allows her to pursue her many interests. And money can take on an added dimension when it is plentiful. When Diana is not limited by financial constraints, she can, if she wants, broaden the scope of her solitary pleasures. A country house, membership in a health club, a ceramics course, and so on are some of the things she can enjoy.

In love relationships, Diana insists on being absolutely independent financially. Sometimes complicated arrangements for bill payments and household expenses have to be made with her partner. Since she is clear-cut about what she wants and needs, this is usually able to be worked out easily by both parties. If Diana is about to be married, she may want a prenuptial agreement that spells out who gets what if the marriage dissolves. She is very careful about keeping her financial autonomy intact. Even with a live-in lover, she has all her legal financial rights at her fingertips in case she needs them.

Along with retaining her own name after marriage, Diana keeps her checking account, savings account, and securities and investments separate from those of her husband. In a case of joint ownership (such as real estate), financial distribution after a marital breakup is spelled out by contractual arrangement.

Having her own financial resources is very important to Diana. It is essential for her well-being to feel autonomous. Feelings of financial self-sufficiency are a source of strength and power.

Financial dependence, for Diana, means powerlessness and feelings of helplessness. But since she has a good understanding of her needs, she rarely gets into this kind of situation.

Love Relationships

Diana gets involved in low-key love relationships rather than intense love affairs. She has a tendency to drift in and out of short-term relationships, usually with a partner who is immature or self-centered. Diana herself is not interested in commitment or in taking responsibility for nourishing the partnership.

Rather than a torrid affair, Diana wants to be part of a couple for the companionship it provides. Her lover or husband is more of a friend than a sexual partner. Since she is basically asexual in nature, Diana's love relationships center around activities that will complement her self-imposed isolation. Diana is very aware that she needs affection and warmth, but she isn't always able to choose a partner who will give her that.

When Diana's love relationship *is* working well, she and her partner can easily establish a routine in which each person has the time they need to themselves. Privacy is respected and so are the rules of the household which both have established. If Diana wants to work by herself at her computer on Saturday mornings, she feels free to do so without having to explain or justify her reasons.

Diana does not feel the need to nurture her partner or the relationship. At times she can be tender or loving, but her fierce independence makes it hard for her to give full emotional support. She believes that people (herself included) should rely mainly on themselves for the sustenance they need. Since she lives by this code, she expects her partner to do likewise.

In a healthy, positive relationship, Diana will be able to balance her need for solitude with whatever the partnership requires. For Diana, a harmonious love relationship is one in which she feels comfortable about leaving temporarily to do her own thing. Being constantly involved with the relationship causes stress and anxiety for her.

At first, new love relationships can be difficult for Diana. It may seem strange to some potential partners, but Diana has accepted this need for seclusion as part of her deep inner being, and she is comfortable with it.

Diana doesn't fall head over heels in love. Rather, it's a steady, slow process of getting to know and like the other person. Intimacy, for Diana, is not the sexual act. It is the fond and amicable understanding of two people who feel that they are kindred souls. Getting closer, for Diana, means getting to know more about the other person, but not necessarily helping to solve problems or be a helpmate.

Diana is quick to encourage her partner to be independent. "You can do it!" is her watchword. She sloughs off any signs of emotional dependence on her partner's part. If Diana feels that her partner is constantly using her as a sounding board instead of dealing directly with the problem, Diana will insist on detaching herself from the situation.

In general, Diana relies on her partner mainly for companionship. The love relationship allows her to have a person in her life that can witness her cares and concerns with love. It also gives her the opportunity to exchange feelings and ideas with another human being for whom she has a strong affinity.

Diana leaves love relationships easily—sometimes too easily. Very often she is out the door before anything has a chance to get started. If Diana is unable to satisfy her needs for privacy at the beginning of a relationship, she may discard it immediately. If Diana is married, she feels no compunction to work things out if things aren't going her way.

Finding Happiness

Diana is most content in solitude. It is her way of centering herself. In quietude she can inwardly process the day's activities or think about her life path. Whether she's meditating or walking in a snowy woods, she is drawing her psychic energy inward instead of expending it. For Diana's well-being, it is important to establish a routine that allows her the time and seclusion she needs to refresh herself. Far from being self-absorption, the emotional need to withdraw every now and then from the everyday world of striving and accomplishment, of coming and going, is a deeply felt need that must be valued and accommodated.

Diana *can* find happiness with a partner, family, children, but it is not an easy road. Finding the right person, someone who understands her nature, can be tough. A partner who doesn't feel threatened by her seemingly long stretches of isolation would probably be ideal. She needs a person who is sensitive enough to realize that Diana's aloneness is her way of energizing herself and renewing her spirit, not a rejection of her partner.

Peace and happiness are synonymous in Diana's vocabulary. The serenity that can be found in sharing experiences with a friend, the tranquility of a water lily pond, the quiet beauty of a summer night's sky—these are some of the things that can bring contentment to Diana.

Feelings of independence and power are also sources of happiness. Both inner and outer autonomy are necessary. In the inner realm, Diana's sense of herself as an autonomous woman gives her courage. And in the outer realm, when she can direct the energies she has accumulated in solitude to real accomplishments in the world, she feels powerful. For example, if she spends time alone meditating on the direction she should take in a faltering love relationship and then actually goes ahead and acts on her conclusions, she feels powerful and happy. Instead of succumbing to helpless hesitation or inaction, she has forged ahead by using her own energies.

Paradoxically, she also knows when to let things be, when the time does not seem right for action. Diana understands that her ability to wait is a source of power to her. In nonaction she finds strength.

Erika, the Wise Woman

Whether Erika is eighteen or eighty, she embodies the qualities of the wise woman, the woman who temporarily withdraws for analytic thinking to connect with her deep Inner Feminine. She is simultaneously Daughter, Mother, and Grandmother Wisdom, a woman whose sharp perception can pierce stereotyped societal thinking. Erika is a healer—physically and mentally. She awakens self-healing powers in others, and she commands respect because of her life-affirming, meditative, contemplative, and centered ways. She is concerned with comfort and the relief of suffering. But unlike Belinda's protective and maternal caring, Erika cares for and honors destiny and the journey of life as a cycle of self-transformation.

Erika's intuition is her intelligence, and she responds to it as a power that can be used to discover fate—her own and that of others. Psychic powers and intuitive knowledge make her very aware of her own rhythms.

Erika realizes what it means to be an "essential" woman, and she knows how to love and live the feminine that is her essence. She is receptive and nurturing and uses her powers to free women from their misguided perceptions about their own femininity. Her wisdom and intuition can cut through conscious and unconscious delusions about the process of femininity and the nature of womanhood. In her compassionate aspects, she makes it a point to help other women gain intuitive knowledge of their destiny and growth.

In her negative aspects, Erika's powers can literally petrify her; they can solidify her and turn her to stone. She may attempt to control the fates and their actions—or try to infuence them instead of opening herself to their messages. Then she may harden and become grandiose and self-righteous. As a helper and a seer, she may be swept away by her own feelings of self-importance. She may become an eccentric hag who spreads her insight like sour wine in places where it is not wanted or appreciated.

At times her wisdom can denegrate into the realm of old wives tales instead of bringing gifts from the vessel of her true feminine, from an understanding of the mystery and grandeur of existence. Erika must keep her strong connection to the cosmos, seeing it as both a cycle and an arrow. It is only in connection to this process of renewal that Erika can return, again and again, to her *own* feminine powers of renewal.

Erika derives her feminine power from an understanding of unobstructed self-healing and self-transformation. At her most feminine, she experiences herself and her fate as one motion toward wholeness.

Friendships

Erika brings a quiet, reflective wisdom to her friendships. She is intuitive and responds to the deepest needs of her friends. She is centered in a calm collected way and is not easily distracted by the sometimes hectic life around her. Erika exudes peace. Since she is not easily shaken by events or situations, she can easily tap her own most profound resources. Dedication and courage are her bywords, and friends trust her good counsel to guide them in their own self-change. Erika is concerned with the spiritual and often helps friends to become more aware of their higher nature. She is always ready to guide a friend through an experience or situation so that its inner authentic meaning shines through. She exposes all that is hidden, so that transformational forces can do their work. Erika confronts all that is old and stale and can offer a friend new connections and new pathways.

Erika is a friend you can count on to help you explore the depths of life and to experience a higher self. She dispels the darkness and serves as a catalyst so that luminous understanding is possible. Erika reaches out from a harmonious and beneficent self to examine the shadow places so that dissatisfaction and setbacks can be recognized and overcome. She helps to heal psychic wounds so joyousness can prevail. And when anxiety and doubts are dispersed, Erika is there to help focus on the present and to trust in the process of renewal.

Whether it's a question of forging ahead in a job or a relationship or time to renounce existing goals and plans, Erika's friendship and guidance will cut away all that interferes with new growth and self-renewal. She helps prepare the way—with patience and perseverance—and through her restorative powers and influence, balanced growth is assured.

Erika does not have a vested interest in dispensing her wisdom. Compassion and knowledge are in her nature, and she derives her power from making them available. She guides her friends in the same way she guides herself—outer action is based on inner reflection. Scattered energy is reined in, unclear motivations are made clear, feelings are acknowledged, and the focus of contemplation is turned on experiencing the true present.

If Erika is your friend and Guide, she will provide you with wise energy that can help you free yourself from self-destructive habits or relationships, help bring you out of a depressed or self-absorbed state, or help deliver you from tensions, uncertainty, and obstructions. Erika teaches how to depend on your own inner guidance— and to act from deep inner convictions.

Erika's friendship and guidance may involve a movement ahead and progress, a letting go of old habits and patterns, or it may mean maintaining a "let it be" attitude, taking time to do nothing but submit and surrender, time to wait and watch. Erika's life quest is a search for wholeness. She is attuned to the cyclical nature of the universe, and joys and tribulations are seen as stages of personal growth on life's path.

Erika is very involved with self-transformation—both her own and her friends'. Spiritual prosperity is important to her. But she is wise enough to know that wisdom is not something you can go out and get. It is not a goal to be achieved. Wisdom is something that has to come to you. And Erika has faith in and trusts life to bring what is needed.

Erika believes that by directly contacting the *spirit* of a friend rather than their outward personality, real communion between the two can be achieved.

Work

Erika enjoys work, especially if it is what she considers "righteous" work—the healing professions, working on animal rights issues, as a nutrition counselor, a teacher, astrologer, etc. All would suit her nature well. She has an innate ability to see and understand what people need, and she brings together the forces that are necessary for physical and mental healing to take place. Certain people give off a life force that promotes healing, and Erika is one of those people. Erika is aware of this, and in her work she wants to use this ability as fully as possible.

Erika offers guidance. She is wise, and her compassion is boundless. In her work, Erika derives her power from being able to see the future so that successful action can be taken. She can help examine and explore experiences so that decisions are made effortlessly and from the heart.

In Erika's work, nothing is hectic. Obstructions, uncertainty, and lack of progress are met with perseverance and mindfulness. Erika discards all that is trivial and concentrates on taking the steps that are needed to get the job done. Erika is more concerned with work for its own sake, rather than getting recognition. Knowing she is someone who can use her wisdom for the benefit of others is its own reward. The fruits of her labors are secondary.

In work, as in other areas, Erika is interested in people's innermost feelings. Her life and her work consist of bringing light into dark areas and mending what has been torn apart.

Money

Erika follows the dictum: "Do what you want and the money will follow." Right action for her means following her true nature. She must feel emotionally involved with her work, and she sees money as naturally flowing from her attunement. Erika has the courage of her convictions and is determined to create financial solidity from a career and investments that ring true. If her money-making efforts can, at times, contribute to society, so much the better.

Generosity comes easily to Erika. She sees no reason to hoard or be stingy about money. Her way of giving provides for refreshing the inner resources rather than providing material comfort. Re-creative enjoyment is often what she's after—and she will give her friends gifts of self-development tapes, etc. Erika spends money on her own personal growth too — meditation retreats, nutrition classes, museum lectures, weekends in the country, membership in a health club, and psychological counseling.

Clothes, cosmetics, and keeping or attaining a youthful look are not of prime importance to Erika. She spends money on looking good, but she doesn't go out of her way to always be dressed in the latest fashions. Erika feels comfortable and secure in her classic style, which never goes out of date.

When Erika has cash flow problems, her faithful cheerfulness and optimism win over feelings of despondency and depression. She trusts that sooner or later life will bring her what she needs. While actively pursuing her financial goals, intuition tells her that good luck and her own momentum will reward her.

Love Relationships

Erika is usually able to see the consequences before she acts. In love relationships she seeks a soul mate — a person with whom she can create a union that survives day-to-day stresses, someone who will flourish throughout a lifetime of care. Erika can foresee a potential partner's strengths and weaknesses, so it is difficult for her to get into a relationship that will not be fulfilling.

Erika needs to live with her partner as if it's the only relationship she will ever have. Instead of having one foot out the door, she is devoted to making it work. Erika always addresses the essential inner nature of things, not the superficial actions. She trusts her innate sensibilities and in dealing with problems, she looks at the emotions and feelings behind the actions rather than the actions themselves.

Erika's love for her partner is strong. She is secure in knowing she can provide the relationship with wisdom and strength. She also gives her partner support without creating dependence. Personal growth is important to Erika, so she allows time and space within the union for separateness. In her ideal relationship, she expects to maintain her own identity, while at the same time merging with her partner.

Balance and harmony in a love relationship are primary for Erika, and maintaining a routine that promotes peace, quiet, and tranquility is essential. Cutting away whatever does not instill a sense of wholeness and groundedness may be necessary at times. It is then that Erika and her partner can take a good look at the elements that are creating disharmony and discontent.

What Erika needs in a love relationship is quiet contentment—and she can get that with a partner who is psychologically and spiritually perceptive and who is attuned to her deep inner needs and desires and his own. For Erika, the benefits of sharing a life together should outweigh the struggles. If they don't she will leave. She would prefer to stay in a relationship for what it gives her, rather than get out of it for what it doesn't. But she will never stay in a relationship that holds no promise.

In love relationships, Erika derives her power from giving intuitive wisdom from the depths of her being. In union with her partner, she is able to tap a wellspring that refreshes and recreates her being. She does not feel that she ever has to bend to her partner's will, but rather that they will reach a consensus born of loving concern.

Finding Happiness

Happiness, for Erika, is an everyday experience. Tranquility and peace are at her fingertips, and wisdom is an available commodity that she can tap when necessary. Erika requires a strong connection to nature's cycle—the weather, seasons, the moon phases. She is very aware of her biorhythms and the influence of her menstrual cycle on her moods and her sexual needs. She is in contact with her dreams and values their messages. All this brings her contentment.

For Erika, happiness means being able to direct her outer world with the insights she gets in quiet contemplation. Erika derives her power from deep inner convictions, and she feels most alive when she is using her wise and intuitive self—whether that is with a partner or friend, her children, at work, or for her own personal growth.

Erika plumbs the secrets and mysteries of life and finds golden opportunities for love, self-discovery, heightened intellectual and emotional awareness, and satisfaction with work. By examining her own deepest thoughts and feelings, Erika is able to actualize her abilities in the everyday world. The combination of inner exploration and outward achievement brings Erika great happiness. When both elements flow smoothly, she is at her best.

Happiness, for Erika, is personal and private, but she is willing to share her experiences with people who are perceptive. Not willing to cast pearls before swine, she gives her wisdom to those who are truly seeking a higher consciousness. When her astuteness is received with understanding, Erika finds the contentment she desires.

4

Putting Your Guides to Work

Putting Your Guides to Work

All of your Guides are available to you all the time. It is just a matter of contacting the one you need and communicating your concerns. In this chapter, you will complete a series of visualizations and learn how to put your Guides to work. It may sound as if they are working *for* you, and in the beginning they will be. Eventually, you will start to feel that they are working *with* you.

Your Guides are not guardian angels, but they do have your best interests at heart in the same way a loving friend does. But more than that, they have knowledge and power that they can transmit to you in the visualizations. A Guide is part oracle, part advisor—she always conveys the truth and helps you to understand how to use it. You can recognize the truth because it is *your* truth. And in the same way, with your Guides' help, you will recognize what is the right action for you. Far from being supernatural beings or vaporous spirits, they are as real as electricity. Their energy can enlighten in a truly meaningful way.

Read the chapter at your own pace. There is no need to rush or push yourself. Take the time to approach the material as you would

Putting Your Guides to Work

a beautiful moon. Look at it. See its aspects. You can return tomorrow night with your inner telescope and investigate it more closely.

These are some of the questions that will be answered in this chapter:

How do I know which Guide I need?

When can I call upon my Guide?

How do I contact my Guide?

How can I benefit from the guidance I receive?

What are some other ways I can experience my Guides?

What if I can't contact or communicate with my Guide?

What if I don't fully understand the guidance given by my Guide?

Can I protect myself from harm? Attract good fortune?

Is there anything special I can do in key periods of my life?

You will begin by finding the Guide you need, learning when to go to your Guide, and learning how to contact your Guide through a series of four separate visualizations: Meeting the Heart; Receiving Power; Mantle of Beauty; and Circle of Friendship. Each of these visualizations is designed to increase Inner Feminine Power as you go along. To derive full benefits from the visualizations, it's necessary to do them in the order in which they appear.

In the second half of this chapter you will learn how to use the Four Directions visualization for crisis situations, Crossover visualization for major breakthroughs, and Receiving a Boon visualization for key periods in your life. You'll also find out how, when, and where to use two all-purpose and all-powerful visualizations that can release tremendous energy. They are called Erika's Wisdom and Opening the Door.

Finding the Guide You Need

As you know, your #1 Guide has the strongest influence on you. She's the one you feel most comfortable with—whether your concerns are about work, friendships, happiness, money, or love. The Helping Guides are the ones you call upon less frequently or not at all. It would be unusual to only rely on or feel comfortable with your #1 Guide. But you need to know which Guide to choose when you need help.

Let's say you have a problem in your love relationship. Your partner wants all your free time to be spent together, but somehow you feel that consulting with Diana isn't what you want to do at this time. It doesn't feel right, for whatever reasons—you feel Diana will understand but won't have much to contribute, or maybe you think you have listened to Diana enough and now it's time to get a new perspective. You want guidance, but you don't know which Guide to get in touch with. You decide that what you need most is to alleviate your anxiety first. In this situation, you feel that Eva can put you at ease. It *feels* as if Eva can give you the support and encouragement you need.

In another example, your #1 Guide is Kendra. You've just adopted a baby, and you find it difficult to balance career and family life. But most important, you think you've lost connection with the nurturing mothering side of yourself. You think of Belinda as the most obvious choice to guide you. But going to Belinda doesn't seem right. You *feel* an affinity with Erika, and the idea of conferring with her at this time is reassuring.

In both of these examples, you have found the Guide you need by allowing your feelings to take the lead. If calling on your #1 Guide feels as if it will satisfy your needs—relieve pressures, unburden you, reduce discomfort, console or calm you, brighten your outlook, guide you in making the correct decision, or clarify an important issue— then get in touch with her. Or, if you feel drawn to one of the Helping Guides, go to that one. The Guide you go to depends on your feelings of affinity to that particular Guide *at the time.* Go to the Guide that feels right for your question, problem, experience, or situation.

If you feel yourself absolutely unable to decide on a Guide, remember that you can always go to Erika. As the wise one, she can impart intuitive wisdom, and her understanding is all-encompassing. Erika is the Guide you can choose when you are unsure or unclear about which Guide you need.

When to Go to Your Guide

You can confer with your Guides as a routine or go to them whenever you need to resolve a problem or answer a question. You can call upon your Guide in a crisis (an acute and distressing situation), or at key periods in your life (such as marriage, the birth of a child, etc.).

As a routine, setting aside a few minutes or more to spend time with your Guide can be done on a daily or weekly basis. If you are the kind of person who enjoys meditation or quiet contemplation at fixed times, then the routine of talking with your Guide every day or once a week will probably be very satisfying. In this case, you can put a loose limit on the amount of time (one minute, five minutes, etc.) or you may want to leave it open-ended.

If you want to consult with your Guide about a problem or ask a question you can do this at any time—as part of a routine or when the need arises. It's possible to go to your Guide for a minute in a crowded subway or classroom. But for the full benefits, contact with your Guide should be made through a visualization, so it's best to set aside enough time to do the visualization and feel its effects. Start with twenty minutes and adjust the time as necessary. The quality of the time is more important, of course, than the quantity— but allow leeway for inner connections to be made.

In crisis situations—job dismissal, confrontation with your lover, ill health, conflicts with teenage children, home relocation, etc.— you can go to your Guide (in a visualization) for practical advice, comfort, and solace. Whether you spend five minutes or an hour with your Guide, the important thing to remember is that you can return as soon as you need to, as often as you want.

Note: There's one very important exception to this: if you *change* Guides and use the same visualization for both Guides, you must always wait twenty-four hours.

During the key periods of your life, your Guide can give you invaluable guidance. Marriage, the birth of a child, divorce, a career or job change, and turning thirty, forty, or fifty years old are all stages of life when extra input is necessary. Everyday concerns and feelings during these rites of passage are intensified and magnified. You may need your Guide to help sort things out and resolve any conflicts. It is at these times that you can call upon your Guide to show you the way.

Here, as in crisis situations, you can go to your Guide for as long and as often as you want and need to (remembering, of course, to wait the necessary twenty-four hours if you change to another Guide within the same visualization).

It is also important to note that at times you will be going to your Guide with good news—the joys and triumphs of a new job, a new relationship, settling in with four stepchildren, or a sudden financial windfall. All these things can be shared with your Guide. Also, each and every one of the Guides has a sense of humor, so don't hesitate to laugh at your foibles as well as commiserate about your sadness or discomfort.

Contacting Your Guide

Contact with your Guide is established through a series of four separate visualizations: Meeting the Heart; Receiving Power; Mantle of Beauty; and Circle of Friendship. In Meeting the Heart you will meet your Guide and ask her a question; in Receiving Power you will receive power that is transmitted by your Guide; in Mantle of Beauty your Guide will give you a mantle to protect you from negative influences; and in Circle of Friendship you will, with the help of your Guide, reach out to others and welcome them into your life.

The series of four visualizations should be done consecutively at first. Meeting the Heart should be completed at least once before beginning the second visualization. Continue in this manner so that you do not begin a visualization before completing the ones preceding it. To derive full benefits from each visualization, the next visualization should not be done on the same day.

Putting Your Guides to Work

This series of visualizations was designed to increase Inner Feminine Power as you go along. Powerful forces are at work here. As you complete each visualization, you will not only receive and accept what your Guide has to offer, you will also build up a reservoir of Inner Feminine Power that will sustain and strengthen you throughout your life.

Begin by setting aside twenty to thirty minutes. This will give you enough time to center yourself and complete the visualization. (A visualization is complete when you receive and accept what your Guide offers you.) The room should be relatively quiet and free of distraction. Soft lighting is helpful. Sit quietly in an upright position and relax your body and your mind. Free yourself from everyday tensions and concerns. Open your heart. Do not *think* of your heart opening, but rather, *feel* it opening. Let go of expectations. Your heart may be opening to what is familiar to you, or it may be opening to what is new and strange. Do not expect that answers to problems will become clear immediately or that all the answers will present themselves. Expect nothing but that you will meet your Guide with an open heart, in an atmosphere that lends itself to positive self-growth. Anticipate nothing but that your Guide will appear and you will be ready to begin a dialogue to open the way.

In the first visualization, you will meet your Guide and ask a question. By its nature, a question that can be answered with a yes or no (such as "Should I get into a sexual relationship with Jerry?" or "Am I *ever* going to meet Mr. Right?") is limited, and so are the answers. Rephrasing the question can address the same issues, while at the same time allowing a more complete answer to be given. The questions above can be rephrased: "If Jerry and I were lovers, what would our relationship be like?" or "Is Mr. Right a concept I want to hold onto, or should I switch gears and be content with what's available?"

Meeting the Heart

Think of a question that is specific. Choose the Guide you need. When you are ready, prepare yourself for the visualization, as previously instructed. It is called Meeting the Heart and is designed so that the heart-to-heart talk with your Guide meets with success.

Meeting the Heart

Relax your body. Close your eyes. You will meet
your Guide in the heart of a fruitful valley. In
the middle of the valley, there is an orchard. And now,
meet your Guide at the entrance to the orchard and
walk inside together.

Look around. Everywhere the fruit is ripe and
deeply colored. At the center of each fruit, there
is a seed. Take time to notice your surroundings. (Pause.)

Your Guide understands that you have come here
to ask an important question. To receive an
answer, you must first concentrate on the heart space.
With each inhalation, focus on your heart space.
With each exhalation, let go of tension. (Continue for
about two minutes.)

By concentrating on the heart space, you are now
aware of your heart's desire. In your own time, ask
your Guide the question and listen mindfully to
what she says. Continue to spend as much time with
your Guide as you need to. (Pause.)

When you are ready, receive and accept the answer
and return to your usual awareness. Remember that you
can come back at any time to meet your own heart's desire.

Benefiting from Meeting the Heart

Take time to sit quietly for a few minutes to get the full effects of
your meeting. Feel the impact of seeing and talking to your Guide
for the first time. Was it intense? Low-key? Noncommital? Rich?
Emotionally flat? Vibrant? Was it a dialogue? Or did you do all the
talking? Or did she?

Witness the content of the visualization by replaying the guidance you were given—that is, replay the answer to your question
and any other messages you received. If, in the visualization, your

question has been answered, you can choose to accept the answer or not to accept the answer.

If you think the answer is valuable, you can accept the answer as is, or you can go on to any one (or all) of the following things:

1. Center yourself (now or at some other time) and let your mind elaborate on the answer.
2. Return to your Guide (now or at some other time) by doing the visualization again. This time you can ask other questions pertaining to the answer, or you can ask your Guide to elaborate on the answer.
3. Continue (another day) with the other visualizations in the series.

For example, let's say you met with Belinda in Meeting the Heart and asked, "What is the most compassionate and supportive way of helping my AIDS-stricken friend Richard?" After the visualization, you were able to feel the impact of seeing Belinda for the first time and talking with her about your concerns. Let's say that Belinda has answered your question with specific and practical advice. She then asked you about your feelings. And she tells you to prepare for his anger, a matter you had not considered before.

After the visualization, you were able to get the full impact of the meeting—it was intense and rewarding. Although you were hesitant and unsure at first, you become stronger and more positive because of Belinda's reassuring presence. The fact that it was a dialogue was important to you because you felt that you could both question and respond to her as an equal.

You then went on to accept the answers and to spend a few minutes amplifying them. To do this, you decide to focus on preparing yourself for Richard's anger and on your own feelings of helplessness in the face of it. You don't think it's necessary to return to Belinda for clarification, and you decide to continue with the other visualizations at some other time.

In following visualizations, the same Guide may appear in the same or different forms. If, in your first meeting, Kendra had long dark hair or indistinguishable features, she may very well appear that way again—but she could also show up as a blonde with a large nose. More often than not, your Guide is a felt presence rather than a person, and even such things as a blue light or a rose quartz can be the forms in which she manifests her energies and transmits her power.

> **Note:** If, for some reason, you are absolutely unable to contact your Guide after thirty minutes, go to the list of affirmations at the end of this chapter (page 127) and read the first one. Affirm your willingness to accept guidance. Return to Meeting the Heart on another day and begin again with the Guide you feel an affinity with (it can be the same Guide or a different one). The visualization can be completed once you make contact with your Guide. If your question was answered and you chose not to accept it, return to Meeting the Heart on another day and begin again with the Guide you feel an affinity with. The visualization can be completed once your question is answered and you receive and accept it.

Receiving Power

The second visualization is called Receiving Power. In it you will receive power transmitted by your Guide. On a person-to-person level, power can be transmitted in many ways—it can flow through the fingertips to heal, alleviate pain, or relax muscles; it can shoot out of the eyes to describe the strength of feelings and emotions, or to command attention; and it can radiate from the heart as love. Deep down, we all have the power to heal ourselves and others, the power to know our innermost feelings. We all have the power to love. And deep down, we can transmit that power to others.

In the next visualization, you will receive the power transmitted by your Guide. You may experience it as strong, weak, or intermittent. Each Guide's energy is distinctive and varies from time to time in intensity. For example, Nixa's creative energy will be stronger at certain times than at other times. As in Meeting the Heart, you can accept or reject the power.

The energy transmitted by your Guide is energy that can be stored by you or used immediately. You may need energy now to accomplish something and to refresh burned-out feelings. Harassment on your job or in your love life requires a prompt recharge. On the other hand, you may need to store up energy. Just as a leaf soaks up sunlight to stay green and sturdy, it is also necessary that you accumulate energy.

Choose the Guide whose power you want to receive. If you feel that Eva's power to attract love is what you need, that is who you should choose. If you need Nixa's power to create, go to her.

Here is a list of the primary power that each of the Guides can transmit to you:

♡ EVA	Power to Attract Love
□ KENDRA	Power to Achieve
○ NIXA	Power to Create
☐ BELINDA	Power to Nourish
☽ DIANA	Power to Be Independent
△ ERIKA	Power to Reveal Wisdom

In Receiving Power you will be shown how to receive your Guide's primary power (but you can also transmit other strong energies). Let's see how this primary power can work in choosing your Guide.

Let's say your #1 Guide is Kendra, and you are now drawn to Eva for the Receiving Power visualization. You feel as if you're becoming a workaholic and your power to attract love has faded. You are going to Eva as you would go to a friend you admire, someone who has the knack of attracting love. In the case of a friend, you might say to yourself, "How does she *do* that? I wish I had the hang of it. If it seems so *easy* for her, she must know something I don't." You are choosing Eva to receive the Power to Attract Love.

Similarly, let's say that your #1 Guide is Belinda, and you are drawn to Kendra for Receiving Power. You feel that you're too wrapped up in family life, and you want to go out into the world and accomplish something. You are going to Kendra in the same way you would to a friend who has the natural ability to strive and make things happen. You are choosing Kendra to receive the Power to Achieve.

In this last example, your #1 Guide is Diana, and you are drawn to Nixa for Receiving Power. You feel that your solitary and independent life is rich and rewarding, but is not as satisfying on a creative level as you would like. You are going to Nixa as you would go to a friend who is extremely creative. You are choosing Nixa to receive the Power to Create.

The examples above will help you in deciding what part of your life needs energizing at this time. Then choose the Guide who can give you the power you want.

Prepare yourself in your own time, and begin the Receiving Power visualization.

Receiving Power

Close your eyes, relax your body. Breathe slowly and deeply, and feel yourself unwinding. Feel yourself floating down, down, down. Deep down, picture yourself on a quiet, moonlit beach.

Your Guide _____ (fill in Guide) is there to greet you. She understands that you are here to receive the Power to _____ (fill in appropriate power). Sit with her on the beach. Look up at the moon and notice its aspect. Observe its place in the sky. Be aware of its shimmer on the sea. Understand that the moon waxes and wanes. Know that the moon moves slowly, but it crosses the sky.

Stand facing your Guide. Breathe deeply. Stretch your hands out in front of you, palms up—and almost touch your Guide's extended hands, which are palms down.

Sense the energy flowing from your Guide's fingertips. Feel it as a vibrant pulse. Draw the Power to _____ to you in the same way the moon draws the power of the tides. As you inhale, let the energy fill every cell of your body. As you exhale, let go of any tension.

Continue as long as necessary to fill yourself with the power your Guide is transmitting. (Pause.) In your own time, return to your usual awareness refreshed and filled with energy.

Remember, you can come back to this place of empowerment at any time, and with a different Guide.

Benefiting from Receiving Power

You now have a greater concentration of energy to draw on when you need it. To benefit from Receiving Power, it is necessary to take everything you brought back from the visualization a step further. How can you make use of, let's say, the Power to Reveal Wisdom that you received from Erika? There is no one answer—but there are many questions that will free you from unnecessary constraints and allow you to take right action:

In your visualization, when you looked up at the moon, what was its aspect? Full? Half? Quarter?

What was its place in the sky? Overhead? On the horizon? Midway? Rising? Setting?

Was the moon bright? Dull? Clouded? Dark? Hard to see?

As you felt the Power to _____ coming from your Guide's fingertips, was it strong? Weak? Assured? Hopeful?

As you were drawing the energy to you and letting it fill your entire body, did you sense that there was a place to take this energy later on?

To what place in your day-to-day life can you bring the Power to _____ ? What stands in the way of fully using your newfound power? What more do you need to know to make the Power to _____ a living reality?

Give yourself a few moments to experience the visualization and its benefits as one living, breathing entity. Feel that you and the Power to _____ are moving ahead into the everyday world and that you are going to use your newfound power in exactly the ways you want. There is no need to plot and plan. Simply bring your power into every situation that requires it and trust that your energy will generate everything you want for yourself and others.

Let's say you went to Nixa for the Power to Create. In the visualization, the moon was full, bright, and overhead. Nixa transmitted her energy, which was strong and hopeful. You let the energy fill every cell of your body, and you sensed that you could take this energy into your love relationship later on. Specifically, in your day-to-day life, you felt that you could take Nixa's creative powers into areas that could strengthen the bonds of intimacy between you and your lover. You felt that the issue that stands in the way of using your newfound power is fear of losing your independence. What you need to make the Power to Create a living reality is the ability to *trust* your creative energy.

As you give yourself a few minutes to experience yourself and the Power to Create as one entity, you feel free to move into everyday situations and use your energy in a new way. You see that fear of losing your independence is an unnecessary constraint you have given yourself—and, in a leap of faith, you *trust* that you will create the intimacy you want with your lover and keep your beloved independence at the same time.

In a similar manner, you can benefit from Receiving Power in your own special way, in your own circumstances and relationships.

Note: If there is anything that prevented you from receiving power from your Guide, go now to the second affirmation (page 127). Repeat the affirmation (silently or aloud). Remember that you can return to the visualization at a time that is more favorable.

Mantle of Beauty

As already stated, you will be ready to do the third visualization, Mantle of Beauty, after you have completed the previous visualizations (Meeting the Heart and Receiving Power). In this visualization, your Guide will give you a Mantle of Beauty. Accepting it and wearing it will protect you from negative influences, such as indifference, bitterness, and hatred.

Mantle of Beauty can be used whenever you feel particularly unprotected. Or it can be used on a routine basis so that the process of protecting yourself remains strengthened.

Let's say you go to Diana to receive and accept the Mantle of Beauty. You have been overscheduling your social life, and you need to slow down and be alone. You know your friends will try to intimidate and cajole you into running around with them. You want to protect yourself from your friends' arm-twisting tactics.

In another instance, you have decided to receive and accept the Mantle of Beauty from Kendra. You feel that you need protection on the job because hostility is being directed toward you at work. To feel protected for the week ahead, you make a decision to set aside ten minutes every Monday morning to do the Mantle of Beauty visualization.

The Guide you go to is always the one for whom you feel an affinity at the time. In both of the cases above, you went to the Guide that you felt could give you the protection you wanted.

You can receive the Mantle of Beauty as many times as you need, from different Guides. But remember that you must *always* wait twenty-four hours whenever you change Guides.

Prepare yourself and begin, in your own time, the Mantle of Beauty visualization.

Mantle of Beauty

Close your eyes and relax your body. On the inhalation, take in fresh, clear energy. On the exhalation, let go of all harm. Release anything that can be hurtful or damaging to yourself or others. (Continue for about one minute.)

In time, your Guide will bring you a Mantle of Beauty. It is a cape that will protect you and enable you to complete important life tasks.

Go now to meet your Guide. She is waiting for you in a far-off place. You begin to walk, and after a long time on the path, you arrive at a cottage. In the

rose garden, your Guide is waiting for you. Take time now
to sit with her and talk. (Pause.)

And now, your Guide gives you the Mantle of Beauty. Feel
how soft and lightweight it is. Notice how thickly woven
and strong it is. Receive and accept the Mantle of Beauty.

It is time to put on the Mantle of Beauty. This is your
protection against harm. Wear it now.
Feel how lovingly the mantle protects you. Realize that
wearing it will help you in many ways.

Return now to your usual awareness, secure in the
feeling that you are protected from negative influences.

Benefiting from Mantle of Beauty

The Mantle of Beauty visualization will strengthen your power to
protect yourself. After completing the visualization, try to stay with
the secure feeling of being protected as long as you can. In everyday
experiences, you can return to and draw on this available energy
whenever you want.

Protection from harm, in practical terms, means that your heart,
body, and mind immediately safeguard themselves from negative
influences that can be damaging. Wearing the Mantle of Beauty
represents your ability to do that.

When negative energy (your own or others') is absorbed into
your system, your own natural, healthy energy is interrupted. You
may lose your sense of stability or become depressed and listless and
find it difficult to get things done. Your immune system and the
ability to heal yourself can become weakened.

Knowing and feeling that you can protect yourself in any
experience or situation is what is needed first. After that, one of the
most important ways to empower your protective energy is to learn
to say no. One of the primary tasks for all women is not to let
themselves be imposed upon by demands that take them away from
what is truly important to them. What is most important—and what
is diverting—will be different for each woman, but learning to say
no to being taken away from the things you truly love is a way of

protecting what is valuable to *you*. If may be a seductive love relationship that's taking you away from work you love (or vice versa). Or maybe friends are overly dependent on your advice and comfort, and take you away from discovering what you need for your own self-development. Or it may be your own oversensitivity to family squabbles that's taking you away from shaping the life you want to lead. Whatever your situation is, you (and you alone) know when it is time to say no to what is harmful.

Cloak yourself in the Mantle of Beauty, not to hide or conceal your own nature, but to confirm to yourself and others that you have set limits and boundaries in which your authentic self can live and thrive. This can be done anywhere, anytime.

Note: If there is something that prevented you from receiving and accepting the Mantle of Beauty, go now to the third affirmation (page 127). Repeat the affirmation. Remember that you can return to the visualization at a more favorable time.

Circle of Friendship

When you befriend someone, you can comfort, be supportive, or pitch in. You can help a friend out of a confusing situation in a marriage or give a bit of practical advice about baby-sitters. Almost all of us know how to go to bat for a friend when necessary, even if it is inconvenient.

But really reaching out to others or welcoming them into an embracing friendship is often something that is overlooked in today's fast-paced "me" society. Attitudes are geared toward looking out for number one and being your own best friend. The *chance* to reach out and the chance to welcome is frequently missed. The moment of true connection between people is lost, and it passes unnoticed.

Friendship is genderless. And a friendship bond can exist very strongly between husband and wife as well as between two women. But, again, the chance for true friendship is an opportunity that can be repeatedly passed up, especially when too much emphasis is placed on your own self-improvement or on attaining other goals.

Venus Unbound

It is said that we cannot love others until we love ourselves. While that may be true in its own way, at some point it's necessary to stop concentrating too hard on self-growth. It's time to pass along some of the wisdom you've picked up on the way. The point is not to force-feed enlightenment by cramming it down someone else's throat. The specifics that have helped you might not be enriching for your best friend—but then again they might be richer and more powerful. Reach out.

In the fourth and last visualization, you will reach out and you will welcome in. The visualization is called Circle of Friendship. Instead of going to your Guide or summoning her, you and your Guide will go together into the circle. There are no questions and there are no answers. There is only reaching and welcoming.

Prepare in your own time and begin the Circle of Friendship visualization.

Circle of Friendship

Close your eyes. Take a deep breath and release tension.
Begin to picture a large circle. Understand that the circle cannot be broken. Visualize that everyone you love and care about is standing inside the circle.
See yourself outside the circle with your Guide.

And now, take a few steps forward with your Guide and enter the circle. Close to those you love, there is warmth.
Inside the circle there is a sense of community and a feeling of strength. Take a few moments to experience yourself in the circle. (Pause.)

Now look outside the circle. There is someone in your life right now who wants to enter and share warmth, a sense of community, and a feeling of strength. Picture that person standing outside the circle.

You want to welcome your friend into the circle.
Take a moment now to experience your generous spirit and to release any anxiety.

On an inhalation, breathe in fresh energy into your fingertips. On the exhalation, release energy from your body, heart, and mind. (Continue for about one minute.)

If tension still exists, ask your Guide if there is anything more you need to do to reach out to your friend. (Pause.) And now, reach out to your friend. Open your heart as s/he steps inside the circle. Take a moment to experience how it feels to reach out, welcome, and share. (Pause.)

When you are ready, return to your usual awareness refreshed and invigorated. Remember, you can return at any time to welcome others into the Circle of Friendship.

This visualization completes the Series of Four Visualizations.

Benefiting from Circle of Friendship

Reaching out, welcoming, and sharing is a lot more than sending a Hallmark card. Extending yourself and touching the lives of others in a meaningful way includes being on the lookout for opportunities to be more than merely thoughtful. It means being open and aware of another person's heart's desire—and being open and aware of your own generous nature. In Circle of Friendship, you reach out with fingertips full of energy. Your hand extends and reaches out and welcomes in. When you experience your own generous spirit, tension dissolves. It is impossible to fully feel your loving nature and feel anxiety at the same time. (And it's *possible* for you to deliberately choose to feel love rather than anxiety.)

If, in the visualization, your Guide sensed there was something more you need do to be able to reach out to your friend, consider that now. Perhaps it is necessary to be a little more optimistic. Or you may need to step outside the circle and talk with your friend for a while. In your own time, think about what more you sense you need in order to reach out with a generous spirit.

Daily life presents you with many chances to enter a Circle of Friendship. The friends you now have are a community of people with whom you can share warmth and closeness. In the circle, you have the opportunity, each day, to be empathic, supportive, and unconditionally giving. Choose to be aware of these opportunities. Similarly, reach outside the circle by opening your eyes and heart to those around you. In this way, you will see (in a heartfelt way) what it is you want to do about reaching out to others.

> *Note:* If you were unable to enter the Circle of Friendship and to welcome someone in, go now to affirmation four (page 127). Repeat the affirmation. You can return to Circle of Friendship at a more favorable time.

Basic Guidelines

The basic guidelines for the series of four visualizations that have already been mentioned in this chapter are presented below so that you can see them at a glance.

- The series of four visualizations (Meeting the Heart, Receiving Power, Mantle of Beauty, and Circle of Friendship) are to be done consecutively at first, in the order in which they are listed. Begin a visualization only after you have completed the preceding one at least once.

- To derive full benefits, two new visualizations should not be done on the same day.

- Never change the visualizations in any way (by substituting words, etc.). They are to be done exactly as they stand.

- A visualization is only considered completed when you receive and accept what your Guide gives you. If you do not or cannot receive and/or accept what is given, return to the visualization on another day and begin again with the Guide you feel an affinity with (it can be the same Guide or a different one). The visualization can be completed once you receive and accept what your Guide offers.

- Using the same Guide, you can return to a visualization at any time. If you change Guides (and use the same visualization for both) you must always wait twenty-four hours. For example, if

Erika is your Guide in Meeting the Heart, you can do the visualization again with Erika at any time. But if you decide to then call upon Nixa in Meeting the Heart, it is necessary to wait twenty-four hours.

• If you change Guides *and* change visualizations, no waiting time is necessary. For instance, if Erika is your Guide in Meeting the Heart and you want to do *another* visualization with Nixa, no waiting period is necessary.

• If you absolutely cannot make contact with your Guide after thirty minutes, go to the appropriate affirmation at the end of this chapter and repeat it. Return to the visualization on another day and begin with the Guide you feel an attunement with (it can be the same Guide or a different one). The visualization can be completed once you make contact with your Guide.

For your own information, you may want to make a chart such as the one below. If you write in the date (or a check mark) indicating that you did each visualization, you can easily see which Guides you are contacting. If you return to the same Guide over and over again, examine and explore your affinity to a different Guide. An attunement with each and every Guide leads to feminine unity. Begin a visualization with another Guide only if this feels comfortable.

Similarly, if you like you can make small notes to yourself about what you experienced during the visualization. If accepting the Mantle of Beauty was difficult, you might want to note that. Or if there was something particularly insightful about meeting with your Guide, you could jot that down.

	MEETING THE HEART	RECEIVING POWER	MANTLE OF BEAUTY	CIRCLE OF FRIENDSHIP
EVA				
KENDRA				
NIXA				

	MEETING THE HEART	RECEIVING POWER	MANTLE OF BEAUTY	CIRCLE OF FRIENDSHIP
BELINDA				
DIANA				
ERIKA				

In the remaining section of this chapter, you will be given three visualizations that you can use for specific occasions: Four Directions, for crisis situations; Crossover, for making major breakthroughs; and Receiving a Boon, for key periods in your life.

These visualizations can be done at any time—either before, in-between, or after completing the four visualizations (Meeting the Heart; Receiving Power; Mantle of Beauty; Circle of Friendship). In other words, the occasion determines when you do the visualizations.

And, to end the chapter, you will be given two visualizations that are all-purpose and all-powerful. Those visualizations are called Erika's Wisdom and Opening the Door. The reason that they are presented last is because of the extraordinary amounts of energy they can unleash. For full benefits, it is advisable that you complete the series of four visualizations before attempting Erika's Wisdom or Opening the Door. It is best to begin them when you are familiar with the Inner Feminine Power you have contacted in the earlier visualizations.

Four Directions

The Four Directions visualization is useful in crisis situations.

Everyone knows that in a crisis situation, it's not always easy to think straight. Contacting your Guide under these circumstances may seem farfetched, but talking with your Guide at this time can be helpful in a practical way, as well as emotionally reassuring.

Instead of going to your Guide in a crisis situation, she will come to you when she is summoned. In Four Directions, she arrives armed with questions, not answers.

For this reason it is important to define what a crisis is and understand what it isn't. We'll describe it loosely as more than an ordinary dilemma or predicament. It's not exactly disastrous, but you've reached your wit's end. It feels as if there is no way out of the mess. It's more than being in a pickle—it *feels* like a major calamity. For our purposes, that's a crisis. Your lover has announced he's leaving, you can't pay unexpected bills, you've failed your final exams, family confrontations are escalating, you've lost your job—these are all examples of crisis situations. You feel crushed, and you can either come to a standstill or establish direction and proceed.

> *Note:* Do not attempt to summon your Guide during medical or psychiatric emergencies of any kind. After the emergency has been resolved and completely taken care of by a licensed medical practitioner, you can proceed to contact your Guide. The same goes for experiences of severe trauma such as rape, mugging, house break-in, car crash, etc. Get immediate help from the police. After assistance arrives, you can proceed—in your own time—to contact your Guide.

To do something constructive about the experience or crisis situation, and to alleviate tension in the meantime, you can summon your Guide in Four Directions. Again, the choice of Guide is yours. In the first instance above (your lover has announced that he is leaving), you would summon the Guide that you feel will give you the direction you need. There are no obvious choices—it's a matter of acting from your own gut feelings.

When you need Four Directions, it is here for you, and you can return to it as many times as you need, until the crisis is resolved. Resolve means "to settle." You may have solved the immediate situation (such as escalating family confrontations) by taking action. But to resolve it (settle it once and for all within yourself) takes time.

If you like, you can read Four Directions a few times and learn it by heart. In that way you will have instant access to it without having to go to a book to retrieve it. (Or again, you can read this into a tape recorder, as suggested previously.)

Four Directions

During this time of crisis, your Guide brings you a message. Close your eyes and picture her standing by you. Feel your Guide's presence. Listen to her as she says:

"From the North I bring you strength
        to sort out confusion,

From the East I bring you clarity
        to shed light on your path,

From the South I bring you wisdom
        to see the truth,

From the West I bring you hope
        to see you through the day,

From the center of the Universe,
let the light and love and power
stream forth into this moment."

Benefiting from Four Directions

In times of crisis, find a quiet place to be alone. (If this is not possible, close your eyes and find a quiet place within yourself.) Quiet your mind and body by breathing deeply and completing the visualization. Afterward, stay with the *feeling* that your Guide is standing by you. Continue to feel her presence with you and:

- Center yourself in your own power to sort out confusion.
- Center yourself in your ability to be clear about your situation.
- Center yourself in your capability to be wise and truthful to yourself and others.
- Center yourself in positive energy that is sustaining and optimistic about the future.

Bring yourself to oneness by focusing your mind on the light, love, and power from the center of the universe. Feel it streaming forth into this moment to help you with whatever it is you have to face. Feel light, love, and power fill your heart. Understand that you are your own power to create peace, love, and abundance.

Note: If for any reason you are unable to complete the visualization, go now to affirmation five (page 127). Repeat the affirmation. At a more favorable time you can return to Four Directions.

Crossover

Crossover visualization is useful in making major breakthroughs.

Crossover is a visualization designed to help you in the process of self-transformation. In this visualization you will cross to the other side—but you will take only what you truly need and want. Unnecessary emotional, intellectual, spiritual, and material baggage is left behind. In Crossover, instead of going to your Guide or summoning her, she crosses with you.

Again, choose your Guide carefully. Crossing over with Belinda is very different from crossing with Erika or Nixa—even though the words of the visualization are the same, the experience will be different. Similarly, when you do the same visualization two separate times with the same Guide, the experience varies, but the bond between you and your Guide remains essentially the same.

As previously stated, the visualization is to be used for major breakthroughs. What does this mean? Basically, it means *when you are ready,* a major breakthrough will occur. There's no forcing it, but there are *signs* that it's coming. The signs appear as feelings, not as thoughts. You can sit forever and think you're suddenly going to see the light about things such as how to improve your sex life or how to stop being a sad sack about lack of money. But it's like the watched pot that never boils. Just because you think you are going to have a breakthrough doesn't necessarily mean it's going to happen.

Your feelings will tell you that a major breakthrough is coming. Sometimes it can feel as if you really are at a crossroad, leaving the old behind as you move forward. But between the old habits and patterns and the new, there is a distance to cross. That's the hard part—crossing that transitional space. But once you've left the old, even if the new is infinite or unknowable, there is a feeling of freshness because old connections have been broken and new ones formed. For example, when you decide to leave a dead-end job or a relationship that's never going anywhere, it's a relief. You don't necessarily know what the future holds, but you do feel that you're ready to cross over into new territory.

Major breakthroughs are *major.* They are not daily or weekly events. And they involve large important issues with which you may have been struggling for years—sometimes since childhood.

When it *feels* as if you have come to a major intersection in your life and you feel ready to cross over, you are ready to complete this visualization. When you feel that you are ready to "go the distance," then you are ready for Crossover.

Crossover

Close your eyes. Breathe deeply and prepare yourself to transcend the limits of your past. Ready yourself for tremendous positive growth. On the inhalation, feel that you are expanding your boundaries. On the exhalation, let go of any refusal to proceed. (Continue for about one minute.)

Picture yourself at a crossroads. You are at a major shift and breakthrough in your evolvement. Your entire life lies behind you. At this time, you are standing with your Guide. She counsels you to take a look at the past, with all its trials and tribulations, with all its joys and triumphs. Look at everything it took to bring you to this place. (Pause about two minutes.) Now acknowledge and release it.

On the other side of the crossroads lies abundance and prosperity. Visualize the sun's rays shining on the crossroad and beyond. Darkness is behind you.

And now, with your Guide, cross over to the other side. Bring with you the power to integrate new energy. Bring with you the power to shed light into the parts of your life that have been denied.

Putting Your Guides to Work

When you reach the other side, realize that you have
separated from refusal to form the life you want to lead.
(Pause.)

And now, spend time with your Guide in an act of courage.
Confirm that you are the source of power and bountiful energy
to cross over into new realms of happiness and comfort.
(Pause.)

Return now to your usual awareness filled
with confidence and new energy.

Benefiting from Crossover

Leaving the old behind can be fairly easy, but facing an unknown
future without your usual props can be intimidating. It seems as if
all you've been, seen, and done can no longer be used in the same
way as before—but still there is no urge to turn back.

After completing the visualization, give yourself time in everyday
life to fully experience the change in yourself. If you find yourself
automatically reacting with distrust to new feelings and thoughts
about your capabilities, pause and reflect on the life you want to
lead (not on the life you've led). Then picture yourself, newly
capable, actually leading that life. Whatever is involved in your
breakthrough—whether it's a career change, a new physical self-
image, or recovering from alcoholism—begin to trust the person
you now are, not the person you were.

In the visualization, you separated from refusal to form the life
you want to lead. This doesn't happen overnight, but little by little
and day by day, you can begin to be the person you've always
wanted to be and do the things you've always wanted to do. What
is needed here is to *believe* in yourself as the source of power and
bountiful energy, to believe that you can shed light on the parts of
your life that have been denied. It takes an act of courage to confirm
this to yourself.

Your Guide can be of great help to you as you transcend the
limits of your past. Call on her whenever you need to. She is the one
who is standing by you in the visualization, and she can help you at
any time.

Remind yourself that you've crossed over and left behind the old self that kept telling you that you could never make it. As your "impossible" dream starts to happen, life will call upon you to rise to the occasion. You may have to give the new you more attention. You may have to study harder at school, or concentrate more at work, or control your temper in a love relationship, or give more thought to how you look.

Do whatever is necessary, always remembering that you have already crossed over with your Guide.

Note: If you were unable to cross over with your Guide, go now to affirmation six (page 127). Repeat the affirmation. When you are ready, on another day, return to Crossover.

Receiving a Boon

Receiving a Boon is useful during key periods.

Boon may sound like a strange word, and it is. But there is no other word that can be substituted. A boon is like a benefit, a blessing but not exactly. It's that "extra advantage" that brings good luck. Few people were born with a silver spoon in their mouth, but there are other inheritances. We can be blessed with other advantages such as good looks, intelligence, a sense of humor, athletic ability, style, an artistic sensibility, etc., which often give us an edge in competitive situations.

During key periods in your life—the time surrounding events such as graduation, marriage, the birth of a child, a divorce, job loss, career promotion or relocation, beginning the care of an aging parent, remarriage and adjusting to an extended family, the death of someone close—a special benefit is necessary. It's almost as if you're saying, "I'm lucky." Most of the time there are plenty of well-wishers when the event is joyous. "Good luck" is heard often at graduations and weddings, and friends usually extend care and concern during a divorce or when you've been fired from your job. But most people do not fully understand how important a given key period is for you. The reason it is called a key period is that it can open the door to the past and the future. Since it is a turning point and a special time, a boon is the extra help that is needed.

In Receiving a Boon, you will have a benefit granted to you by your #1 Guide. It's a gift of good luck, which you can receive and accept.

Begin Receiving a Boon at your own pace and with your #1 Guide.

Receiving a Boon

Close your eyes. Relax deeply. In a moment
your Guide will come to you from the place of love and
abundance. She understands this is a very special time
for you, and she is bringing a gift.

Prepare yourself to receive what she has to offer.
Open your mind and heart to the colors of the rainbow.

Begin to feel your Guide's presence. See her moving toward
you. When she is near, she gives you a red, red scarf.
It is the gift of life and love. You take it
and put it on. She says, "I bring you good luck, happiness,
and comfort. Accept your good fortune." Begin to feel
yourself accepting what she offers. (Pause.)

And now, thank your Guide. It is time to leave.
Return to your usual awareness, bringing with you
the gift of life and love.

Benefiting from Receiving a Boon

To get the most benefits in this key period of your life and beyond, simply center yourself in the positive feeling that all is well. Optimistically look forward to your new situation and *expect* that good things will happen to you. Even if the situation seems overwhelming or anxiety ridden, even if you have to suddenly cope with death, divorce, or job loss, and even if you are confronted with problems that seem unsolvable—always move toward *hopeful anticipation*. That doesn't mean that you haphazardly hope for the best. It means you anticipate and count on good luck and happiness and comfort from within to carry you through any situation. You now possess the gift of love and life. And nothing can take that away from you. If you ever lose connection to that feeling, reach for it as you would reach for the red, red scarf. Wear it, for it is yours.

In the jubilant times, such as a graduation, marriage, the birth of a child, a job promotion, the same practice applies, only here there is not as much negativity to overcome.

You now have the gift of life and love. Count on your ability to use it creatively. Count on good luck, now and in the future. Rely on yourself for happiness and comfort.

Alternate Visualization

The gift of life and love is the primary gift your Guide can give you. In the above visualization it is represented by the red, red scarf. During key periods, your Guide can bring other gifts. The colors below will show you the different boons you can receive. Simply substitute a chosen color for the red in the visualization and receive the corresponding gift.

Color	Boon
Red, red.	the gift of hope and love, as well as good luck, happiness, and comfort
Orange	the gift of freedom from limitation, as well as good luck, happiness, and comfort
Yellow	the gift of self-control, as well as good luck, happiness, and comfort
Green	the gift of health and vitality, as well as good luck, happiness, and comfort
Blue.	the gift of poise and serenity, as well as good luck, happiness, and comfort

Color	Boon
Purple/violet.	the gift of purposefulness, as well as good luck, happiness, and comfort

Note: If for any reason, you were unable to receive and accept the boon from your Guide, go now to affirmation seven (page 127). Repeat the affirmation. At another time, return to the visualization.

Erika's Wisdom and *Opening the Door*

Erika's Wisdom and Opening the Door are two visualizations that are all-purpose and all-powerful. They can be used at any time and in dealing with any problem or issue (large or small). Both visualizations can release tremendous energy. Because of this, and also to derive full benefits from the visualizations, it is advisable that you complete the series of four visualizations before attempting Erika's Wisdom or Opening the Door. In this way you will have some acquaintance with the strength of your Inner Feminine Power—and it will not surface in a way that could be alarming.

Completing either or both of these visualizations on the night of a full moon will increase the benefits.

In Erika's Wisdom you will go to Erika for the wisdom she offers. It can manifest itself in many ways, but it is always extremely potent. When you are ready, prepare yourself. Sit quietly for a few minutes. Relax. Still your mind and quiet your fears. Open your heart. Now you are ready to begin Erika's Wisdom at your own pace.

Erika's Wisdom

Relax and breathe deeply. You are fully relaxed.
Now allow yourself to go deeper, into unexplored territory.

Deep in this free-floating world, there is an image of a wise old woman named Erika. Soon you will meet her and receive the benefits of her wisdom.

Now begin to move toward the wise old woman and her wisdom. Begin to let go of everything that is holding you back. Begin to understand that your own inner wisdom is about to be revealed to you.

Imagine that you are at the bottom of a mountain. At first you can't see a way to go up, but then you notice a narrow path. You climb the path, higher and higher. It is hard at first, but as you continue it becomes less strenuous.

When you reach the top, you see the wise old woman's house. She is there in the garden waiting for you.

Now begin your visit. There is no need to hurry. Take time to find out everything you need to know. (Pause.)

Now it is time to go. Thank the wise old woman for her guidance. Leave the place and walk down the mountain path. When you reach the bottom, open your eyes.

Note: If you were unable to complete the visualization, go now to the eighth affirmation (page 127). Repeat the affirmation. At another time, return to the visualization.

In Opening the Door, what you see, do, feel, and think may be familiar or it may not. Again, Opening the Door is a powerful visualization. Prepare yourself by sitting quietly for a few minutes. Relax your body. Still your mind and quiet your fears. Open your heart. You are ready to begin Opening the Door in your own time.

Opening the Door

Close your eyes and find a relaxed place. Breathe deeply. Imagine that you are going down a long, winding staircase. Go down slowly. When you get to the bottom you see a door. Above the door you read the word *feminine.*

In your pocket you have a key to the door. Take out the key, unlock the door, open it, and go through.

Begin to explore your surroundings. (Pause.) Go a little farther. There's no need to rush; take your time.

Look around at everything. Is there anything you would like to touch or hold? Is there anything far away that you would like to get closer to? (Pause.)

It will be time to leave soon, but you can return whenever you like. Is there anything that you want to bring back with you now? (Pause.)

It's time to come back. Go through the doorway, close the door, and go back up the steps. When you get to the top, return to your usual waking reality and open your eyes.

Note: If for any reason, you were unable to complete the visualization, go now to affirmation nine (page 127). Repeat the affirmation. You can return to the visualization at another time.

This chapter will help you evaluate relationships or a career and give you the opportunity to progress in your own growth and to befriend others. There's really no end to the potential it can present. When the visualizations are completed with purity of heart and courage, Inner Feminine Power becomes more and more a reality.

Now, as you come to the end of Part One, here are some practical ways that you can broaden the ways in which you work with your Guides. Any one or all of these can be incorporated into your life—but only if it feels like a natural outgrowth of *your own experience* with your Guides. If you feel comfortable with an idea, try it. But go along only with what agrees with your own personal enlightenment.

Notes to Yourself

Keep notes to yourself in a notebook or a diary. Writing down impressions, insights, and messages from your Guide can be extremely helpful in keeping track of your progress or as an aid to memory. Whether you have a natural inclination to express your experiences in written form or just want to jot down a few words or phrases, you'll have a record of your inner journey. If you're artistic, drawing a diagram might be an interesting addition.

Dreams

It is possible to take your Guide with you into your dreams. The idea is that you have double your normal power—you and your Guide—to confront and conquer whatever is threatening you, to explore the nature of issues that remain unresolved in your waking life, or to replay a real-life experience.

Before going to sleep, summon your Guide and tell her you want her to appear in your dream to help you solve your problem—or help in some other way. Mention the problem or issue on which you want guidance. After waking, write down what you recall of any dreams in which your Guide appeared.

Sometimes this technique works, sometimes it doesn't. If it doesn't work, try again. People who are attuned to their dreams on a daily basis can often bring this off—and they find it beneficial. If bringing your Guide into your dreams is something that appeals to you, there are several good books on the subject of lucid dreaming that will give you detailed information on how to go about it.

Group Visualizations

You can do a visualization with a friend or as part of a group—after you have previously completed the visualization alone. (Again, remember that the series of four visualizations must be done in the order they appear in the book. Other basic guidelines on page 112 also apply.)

The value of doing the visualizations with another person is that sharing the experience very often loosens emotional constraints. (Of course, it can also have the opposite effect.) To obtain maximum benefits, the visualizations should be done only with a trusted friend with whom you feel strong inner attunement. Remember that in group situations the Femininity Assessment Quiz and a description of the Guides' attributes is a prerequisite to completing any visualization.

Erika's Wisdom and Opening the Door are especially powerful in a group and on the evening of a full moon.

Affirmations

Affirmations are positive statements designed to turn fearful, negative beliefs into positive ones. When the mind is filled with positive thought and the heart is filled with positive energy, progress can be made.

The affirmations below are useful for times when you are unable or unwilling to receive and accept what your Guide has to offer in the visualizations. Each affirmation is numbered, and a note in the text explaining each visualization directs you to the appropriate affirmation below. Repeat each affirmation slowly to yourself (silently or aloud).

1. I am willing to be guided by my own courage and strength.

2. I am in touch with the tranquil, creative power within.

3. My own life force and its self-healing properties surround and protect me from harm. No other shield is necessary at this time.

4. I am able to mirror the heart of a friend by showing my own heart.

5. I am willing to give myself all the help I need.

6. I have arrived at an intersection that can be crossed when I am ready.

7. Difficulties that prevent me from accepting what is offered are dissolving into nothingness. Good fortune is mine.

8. The power to love is in my heart; the power to release hesitations and fears is in my mind.

9. I am the creator of my life, in touch with my energy, courage, and resources.

5

Love Powers

In each of the visualizations, one Guide helped you with issues surrounding work, money, friendships, love relationships, and finding happiness. In this chapter you will concentrate on releasing love powers with the help of two Guides. This double-strength combination is similar to the bonding of two elements into a compound. When two hydrogen atoms [H] are combined with one oxygen [O] under the right conditions, water [H_2O] is created. Likewise, you will combine your #1 Guide with a Helping Guide to form one effective unit. This combination is your Guide pair.

To begin, let's review the symbols for each of the Guides, and then look at examples of how they can be combined.

♡ Eva
□ Kendra
○ Nixa
☋ Belinda
☽ Diana
△ Erika

Let say □ Kendra is your #1 Guide, and ♡ Eva is the Guide you have chosen as your Helping Guide. Putting □ Kendra first, and then your Helping Guide ♡ Eva, the combination in symbols is □ ♡ .

If ☽ Diana is your #1 Guide and △ Erika is the Helping Guide, the combination is ☽ △ .

The chart below lists all the possible combinations between #1 Guides and Helping Guides. As you can see, it is possible to have the same Guide as your #1 Guide *and* as your Helping Guide. For instance, if your #1 Guide is △ Erika, you can also choose Erika as a Helping Guide. The combination, in symbols, is △ △ . Combining your #1 Guide and the same Helping Guide for releasing love powers has very strong positive and negative aspects, depending on which Guide is chosen.

HELPING GUIDES

	♡ EVA	□ KENDRA	○ NIXA	▫ BELINDA	☽ DIANA	△ ERIKA
♡ EVA	♡ ♡	♡ □	♡ ○	♡ ▫	♡ ☽	♡ △
□ KENDRA	□ ♡	□ □	□ ○	□ ▫	□ ☽	□ △
○ NIXA	○ ♡	○ □	○ ○	○ ▫	○ ☽	○ △
▫ BELINDA	▫ ♡	▫ □	▫ ○	▫ ▫	▫ ☽	▫ △
☽ DIANA	☽ ♡	☽ □	☽ ○	☽ ▫	☽ ☽	☽ △
△ ERIKA	△ ♡	△ □	△ ○	△ ▫	△ ☽	△ △

#1 GUIDES

Now, to find your Guide pair, combine your #1 Guide with a Helping Guide. You can choose your first Helping Guide, as determined by the Femininity Assessment Quiz—or you can pick the Helping Guide you *want* to guide you in love. On the following pages, each Guide pair will present you with messages to help you love and be loved in the way you've always wanted. (When we talk about love in this chapter, we are talking specifically about love between a man and woman.) To get the maximum benefits from the messages, it is not necessary to apply them to real-life situations and not just to understand them the way you would understand a message in a fortune cookie. Love Powers are only released when you *use* them. And the messages point the way for that to occur.

Getting the messages across to you is the function of your Guide pair—but it is up to you to use what you learn in everyday life. Making the most of your messages needn't be difficult, and it's a knack you'll learn in this chapter.

Preparation

Before you start to work with your Guide pair, it's necessary to do a bit of preparation. In your own time, begin this three-part process in which you:

1. Acknowledge Your Need
2. Encourage Action that Creates a Balance
3. Make Things Happen

Acknowledge Your Need

Love is an abstract concept, a wide-open field. These days it can mean just about anything. And it certainly means different things to different people. That's generally why so much miscommunication and misunderstanding can exist between lovers.

We all *say* we want this or that kind of love at this or that time. But what do *you* really need in order to be fulfilled? What kind of physical, mental, and emotional bonding with a man do *you* want? How much of it do you want? Let's find out.

To make things easier, let's br ak down the strength of your needs into six categories and give them numbers from one to six.

1. Intermittent
   (varies between weak and strong from time to time)
2. Weak

3. Medium weak
4. Medium
5. Medium strong
6. Strong

Take a pad and pencil. Divide a sheet of paper into three columns with the headings: PHYSICAL, MENTAL, and EMOTIONAL. Without stopping to mull it over, quickly write down under each heading as many things as you can think of that you need *from* a man. We're talking here about what you need in terms of physical bonding with a man, mental bonding, and emotional bonding.

Do you need sexual tenderness? Faithfulness? A gregarious, affectionate, and demonstrative nature? Optimism? Sympathy? Support? Sharing of ideas?

Your list can run the gamut. Write down all the things that immediately come to your mind, even if they sound silly at first.

Now turn the paper over and write the same three headings. Under each heading, quickly jot down as many things as you can that you need to *give* to a man. We're talking here about what *you* need to give to a man to create physical bonding, mental bonding, and emotional bonding.

When you're finished, rate each item (on both sides of the paper) from one to six according to the strength of your needs. If, let's say, you've written "plenty of time for sex" under "Physical" and you've given it a rating of six, that's a strong need. If on the other hand, you've given "fidelity" a three, that's a weak need.

The idea here is to acknowledge your needs—what you need *from* a man and what you need to give *to* a man. Some women feel they need to give a man emotional security by being really affectionate and quietly romantic. Others may feel they need to give ideas and energy. Faithfulness, devotion, generosity, and passion are some of the things women may feel they need from men.

We're talking about needs here—the need to give a valuable part of yourself to the man you love and the need to be given kindness, consideration, sensitivity to your sexual desires, etc. in return. You can give this a bit more thought now and add to your list if you like.

The list will give you a basic idea of what your needs are and which ones are strongest. Acknowledge them. Whether or not they are being fulfilled at the moment is not the point. Any feelings of hopelessness or helplessness about satisfying your needs in the future should be put aside for the time being. Simply take time to acknowledge your needs. This is part of the process of preparing yourself to receive messages about love from your Guide pair.

Encourage Action That Creates a Balance

A balanced love life is created by equalizing. In more or less equal measure, you give and get what you need from your partner—emphasizing your strongest needs and paying less attention to the others because they're not that important to you. When you can do this, the rest is relatively easy if you remain centered in your needs. Day-to-day tensions and distractions can often pull you away from needs. But a period of quiet contemplation will bring you back.

Let's say that your lover has been ignoring you for the past few weeks because he's got a frantic workload. What you need to get from him is affectionate words and hugging (not necessarily sex), a shared meal together, and some assurance that he loves you. Those three things are likely to be high on your list of needs for physical and emotional bonding. Let's also say you need to give him your support and tell him you understand how much getting ahead on the job means to him. And your need to give him physical affection—touching and caressing—is also strong.

This is the time to encourage whatever action is necessary to create a balance. Favor and lean toward conduct that will bring about an equilibrium and symmetry. Your love life is literally "in the balance," and it is at this juncture that right action should be encouraged from within.

It is enough for now to feel your own power to encourage action.

Make Things Happen

Of course, we all want to make things happen. But how? Nobody can make love happen, but we *can* create a climate in which it can occur. We can enrich the soil so romance can flourish despite obstacles and frustrations. Once you acknowledge what you need from your lover (and what you need to give), and you encourage action that creates a balance, you can begin to make things happen by projecting your acknowledged needs into the world. It's not necessary to project and direct the energy onto just one person. Let the world know who you are. Why keep it a secret? Why be ashamed of your list of needs? No matter how ridiculous some of those things may sound to you ("I have a strong need for a tall man with a medium hairy body"), if that's what you feel you need for physical fulfillment, then project that to everyone (and never mind that you are presently involved with a short man without hair on his chest). You don't have to say a word. Just *feel* your needs and project the feeling like a light onto a dark sea.

Whether or not you are now part of a couple, project your needs onto the universe. If, for instance, you need to have your ideas taken seriously by your lover, feel it within. Then project *the feeling.* If you need tact and courtesy, feel it within and project it like a light. If you need to give serenity and patience to your man, feel it within and then shine that message into the darkness.

Making things happen is not entirely in your control. If you already have a partner, you may not always be able to get him to understand your needs or how strong they are. No matter how much you may talk about feelings or try to work it out, inner satisfaction and fulfillment can still elude you.

Acknowledge your needs. Encourage action that creates a balance. Feel your needs and project them into the world . . . and love will happen all by itself.

Love Messages

On the following pages, each Guide pair will give you messages to guide you in love. Your #1 Guide is the one who has the strongest influence on you at this time. At some later date, it may be another Guide. (This is a good reason to redo the Femininity Assessment

Quiz periodically. A birthday is an especially auspicious time to do a reassessment.) Begin with your #1 Guide and then choose the Helping Guide that you feel most comfortable with in love matters — the one that can best help you with success in love. Remember, the #1 Guide always comes first. Example: in ひ ○ Belinda/Nixa, Belinda is the #1 Guide.

Then, go to the appropriate section in this chapter to read the message your Guide pair has for you. The headings are listed by Guide pair. After reading the message, go to Releasing Love Powers (page 163).

Your Guide pair may very well give you a powerful message — it's up to you to put it into practice by applying it to relevant situations in everyday life. The message gives direction and opens the way for Releasing Love Powers. It is up to you to give the message serious consideration and take action whenever and wherever it seems appropriate. Later on in this chapter, you will learn to do that.

♡ EVA	□ KENDRA	○ NIXA	ひ BELINDA	☽ DIANA	△ ERIKA
♡ EVA #1 GUIDE	♡ ♡	♡ □	♡ ○	♡ ひ	♡ ☽	♡ △

♡ ♡ Eva/Eva

Eva as her own Helping Guide can be a powerful force. In forming a union with a man, she is doubly interested and active in releasing love powers. She wants to experience mutual discovery with her partners so that together they bring out the best in each other. Subjectivity and passion rather than reason and objectivity rule. Eva relies on herself as her own Guide, and she uses her own definitions of love to interpret and understand her experiences of it — and she rediscovers and recreates herself in the light of her own true nature. To Eva, the lover and the beloved are one identity in two separate people. Her amorous quest very often does not require a Helping Guide other than herself.

♡ □ Eva/Kendra

Eva/Kendra is a strong love combination. With Eva as your #1 Guide, you can rely on Kendra to help make love happen. Most importantly, Kendra can remove obstructions from love's path, and she can overcome resistance. Kendra can cut away illusions so that Eva can fully experience her sexuality. As a Helping Guide, Kendra's clarity can also help Eva understand her need to unite, to form a union with the one she loves. Kendra shows Eva how to actualize love by giving herself fully and *at the same time* honoring her own strong desires. By learning to keep an open channel between these two states, real intimacy is possible.

On the negative side, Kendra may pull Eva away from her heart's desire. She may work too hard at trying to find love instead of allowing it to occur. If Kendra "goes for it," she may find it has disappeared altogether.

Since Kendra is in charge of what she wants, she may try to control Eva's natural inclination to be earthy, lusty, and erotic. She may play down Eva's need to dress provocatively and "strut her stuff." Only by earnestly listening to Eva's communications can a balance be achieved.

Message: True intimacy can be enhanced by knowledge. Trust in your ability to forge ahead and take action in matters of the heart. Focus on your desires and sexual compatibility first—then follow through with clear thinking.

♡ ○ Eva/Nixa

Eva as the erotic romantic and Nixa as the creative romantic can bring inventive play into lovemaking. Whether sexually assertive or passive, Eva and Nixa both believe in experimenting with sexual urges. Sex is never boring or repetitious. And they can only be satisfied with deep intimacy and a compatibility that has many surprises. Eva is sensitive to her own moods and desires, and Nixa complements this by adding a free-wheeling base in which they can flourish.

Neither one of them puts up with false promises from a man or deception of any kind. In starting a relationship, they both want a physical commitment fairly early in the romance. Eva requires her man to be deeply passionate, and Nixa requires that he be imaginative in pleasing her.

Neither Eva nor Nixa cares if a lover is predictable. Fidelity isn't considered a must either. With inspired eroticism as a motivating force, any kind of lasting commitment from a man may turn out to be impossible.

Eva must get the admiration she thinks she needs from men, and Nixa may enjoy the excitement of the moment, but unless there is a dedication to more solid values, the relationship will fizzle quickly.

Message: Sexual compatibility must be grounded by mental and emotional compatibility. Use passion and creativity to express love, as well as strengthen the bond of friendship, faithfulness, and devotion.

♡ ☐ Eva/Belinda

Belinda brings Eva's unbridled passion down to earth—sometimes too much so. While Eva is strongly sensual and erotically inclined, Belinda's sexual intensity is milder and more directed toward simple affection. If Eva rushes headlong into a love affair with a man who is uncaring, Belinda will pull her away with the thoughts of a stable, secure home and hearth.

Eva has little tolerance for a man that doesn't arouse her, but Belinda shows her that sexual differences with a lover can be overcome. Belinda understands that sexual tension can be replaced with harmony when each partner's needs and wishes are carefully weighed.

For Belinda, sex is one way that two people can share and be together—but it is not intrinsically better than other ways of sharing. Eating together, talking, walking, and socializing together are ordinary situations that are also satisfying. Excitement is not necessarily the same as happiness.

At times Eva can be enjoying herself so much that she doesn't pay attention to Belinda. On the other hand, Belinda may exert too much influence and stifle her passion. Balance is required so that Eva's basic nature isn't unreasonably curtailed.

Message: Passion and domesticity can be reconciled by expressing them clearly and directly—each in its own time.

♡ ☽ Eva/Diana

Diana can be a positive influence on Eva's love life, because she brings independence and solitude into it. She has the ability, in quiet moments alone, to review and integrate experiences and situations. When Eva is open to Diana's reflectiveness, she can sort out problems in her relationship and resolve issues within herself. In peace and concentration, Eva can use your insight to refine and improve her love life.

Diana can also help Eva live according to her beliefs and show her how to express her true feelings without being intimidated by her partner. In money matters, Diana's independent attitudes can complement Eva's sometimes extravagant ways, so that money does not become a bone of contention between her and her lover.

Whenever there is turbulence between Eva and her partner, Diana is there to tell her that seclusion and privacy are necessary before trust and integrity can be restored. Whether Eva needs to wipe the slate clean and start again or just change her attitude, Diana can help her get a sense of herself as a separate person.

Message: In quiet, solitary reflection turbulence can be calmed, harmony can be restored, and decisions can be made. Times of privacy are necessary to come to an understanding of yourself as a self-governing woman.

♡ △ Eva/Erika

Erika's astuteness helps Eva understand how sexual differences can be resolved. It's true Eva has a low tolerance for a man who is temporarily impotent or whose responses are slow. If she is in a relationship, Eva usually feels she is well mated, but she has no

Venus Unbound

patience with a man whose affection wanes or is withdrawn. With Erika's guidance, she can blend her sensual appetites with a bit more emotional tenderness. What may be an impossible love situation in Eva's eyes becomes workable in Erika's. She can also learn to tame her jealousy so that it doesn't erupt into stormy disagreements.

The Eva/Erika pair is a strong one. With care and perception, Erika can help Eva turn selfish pleasure seeking into a more stable mix. For her part, Eva is receptive to Erika's insight—but often ignores it. It's hard for her to resist a man who's handsome, even when she knows she's made a foolish choice.

Erika doesn't give advice willy-nilly; her knowledge is soft and subtle, and it's dispensed like nectar. It can easily be overlooked, however, when Eva's hunger for romance takes precedence over creating stability in the relationship. Eva must also remain alert and protect herself from being betrayed or used by a man. For this she must rely on Erika's uncanny intuition.

Message: Depending only on romantic emotions does not always bring the results you have in mind. It is better to temper strong emotions with insight into your own true feelings.

	♡ EVA	□ KENDRA	○ NIXA	▫ BELINDA	☾ DIANA	△ ERIKA
□ KENDRA #1 GUIDE	□♡	□□	□○	□▫	□☾	□△

□ ♡ Kendra/Eva

When Kendra leads the way in matters of the heart, she's strong willed and determined. She also has her mind made up about what she wants in a man. It's usually someone who won't interfere with her vision of life. Kendra charms her partner with ideas, not with being sexy. Her approach to lovemaking is more mental than it is sensual—and she doesn't take a long time deciding on a partner who will fit into her plans.

If a man is quick to reach out for love, she can just as quickly develop a condescending attitude toward him. But once Kendra and her partner establish an ongoing relationship, she needs Eva's advice to guide her in matters of passion. Kendra is never overly sensitive, and it's easy for her to be objective about love. But it's not as easy for Kendra to be romantic. She wants to protect herself against extremes of emotional states. While Kendra can fall in love and marry Mr. Right, she's not quite sure how to fan the flames of passion. Eva can help Kendra understand the subtle ways in which love can grow stronger through mutual pleasure with her partner.

If Eva's guidance is taken lightly or dismissed, Kendra can be left with a relationship that is predictable and fulfills social needs, but lacks passion.

Message: A partnership between a man and a woman cannot be reduced to a basic formula. When love enters the picture, it is necessary to yield to your own passionate nature instead of taking control. Sexual compatibility can take time, but can only be attained with flexibility and tenderness.

□□ Kendra/Kendra

Kendra is a #1 Guide as well as her own helper here. This puts constraints on love. Without someone to temper her strong will, she can only rely on her outgoing nature to seek out love. She has disowned the Helping Guides that bring her the satisfaction inherent in looking at things from another viewpoint. With no one to question and confront Kendra with fresh insight, there can only be suffering. Without another perspective to counteract a one-dimensional approach to love, there can only be limitation and pain.

Once Kendra recognizes the need and wisdom of a Helping Guide, she can restore harmony. By an act of will, she must pick the Helping Guide she feels most in attunement with.

□○ Kendra/Nixa

Kendra/Nixa can be a powerful combination when it comes to love. With Nixa's imaginative spirit, Kendra can make the most of her relationship. While she always finds endless possibilities for having fun with her lover—taking vacations, sports activities, etc.—when it comes to emotional intimacy, Kendra's not on such solid ground. Here she needs Nixa to pave the way. Nixa can teach Kendra to *experience* her love rather than controlling its direction (or trying to control her lover).

Kendra's objectivity can slow her down in love relationships—so much so that she gets bogged down in reality instead of letting herself fall in love with abandon. If she doesn't heed Nixa's guidance to break away from her analytical ways, love can lose its liberating power.

Since Kendra hesitates when confronted with the unpredictable, she may, at times, be wary of the choices Nixa presents. And Kendra's reasonableness limits her to experiences and situations that aren't too far-out or overly emotional.

When Kendra wants to start a new relationship, she can look to Nixa to make new connections, establish new ties, and show her how to move around and mix in social situations to attract wise-choice men instead of foolish-choice ones. Nixa presents an imaginative point of view, one that stresses a greater need for inventiveness and originality than Kendra is used to.

Message: Ambition has its place in finding love. Imagination has its place in keeping it. But it's not as necessary to keep love in its place as it is to let it soar freely.

□ ♅ Kendra/Belinda

Since hearth and home, marriage and children, are what Belinda is all about, she can help with Kendra's ambition to create a comfortable home for herself and her partner. But the Kendra/Belinda bond is a weak one, because Kendra's energy veers away from domesticity. To Belinda, sentiment is a requirement for romance, whereas Kendra is turned off by whatever isn't precise and clearheaded. Emotions, even in a love relationship, are not primary to Kendra.

Basic differences aside, Belinda can help Kendra nourish and nurture love. In her own way, Kendra can apply the principles of providing, caring, and protecting. Working together, Kendra's strength and Belinda's trusting nature can create a more harmonious environment—one that encourages trust, patience, and a wholesome family life. Kendra *is* optimistic and sympathetic, and Belinda can help her bring those qualities home (literally and figuratively).

Kendra is also strong willed, and her willingness to adapt her ways of being or bend to her partner's desire is almost nil. If, in her tendency to plunge ahead, she discounts Belinda's help, she may find herself incapable of true compassion. But Kendra is smart, and if Belinda presents her case in a reasonable way, Kendra can give her love relationship the attention it needs. By an act of will, Kendra can become more caring, considerate, and responsive in a genuine way.

Message: A love relationship needs true compassion to survive. Patience and understanding promote true intimacy, but courage and ambition are also necessary for it to survive and flourish.

☐ ☾ Kendra/Diana

Kendra and Diana working together on releasing love powers can be very positive. Kendra is directed outward in getting and keeping the man she wants, while Diana is directed inward—she follows her own inner convictions and isn't influenced by what other people think. If Kendra allows Diana to guide her in the ways of love, she will be able to drop her guard a bit and observe her feelings. Instead of being concerned with appearances, Kendra can allow herself to look within at her true emotions. Kendra knows what's on her mind, and Diana can help her understand what's in her heart.

Kendra is always on the go, and Diana shows her the importance of slowing down, taking time to be introspective in a feeling way. Kendra wants to make love workable, and Diana gives her encouragement to examine her emotional involvement.

Kendra makes plans and reviews and reorganizes the logistics of her love relationship. Diana teaches her the necessity of exploring and integrating he feelings into her love life.

Kendra is smart enough to understand the importance of Diana's guidance, but she'll disregard or ignore it when her social life gets frenetic. These are the times when Kendra needs Diana most to balance her hyperactivity and restore harmony.

Message: Focusing on true feelings and inner convictions is necessary for a relationship to grow. Outer appearances and inner values go hand in hand to satisfy deep desires. Times of quiet contemplation restore balance and create harmony.

□ △ Kendra/Erika

The achiever and the wise sage are unbeatable when it comes to love. Erika's deep insight and Kendra's ability to follow through combine to provide a solid basis for lasting romance. Accepting Erika's foresight and shrewdness, however, requires Kendra to go to her with humility. Kendra, for all her perception, must be willing to open herself to a discerning, learned authority who is erudite and knowledgeable. Erika is an oracle, and in matters of the heart she has deep and profound knowledge to impart. Kendra is well-informed, but Erika is a luminary who can present love's path in a way that shines light in all its dark corners. Kendra must then give in to Erika's foresight rather than use her own strong will to find or make love happen.

Kendra must go to Erika as a seeker of love, not as a headstrong achiever. In modesty, and with a certain amount of humbleness, it is necessary for Kendra to acknowledge that love is a matter not entirely in her control. Powerful universal forces are at work, and they cannot be objectified or categorized. Erika's lesson is wisdom, and Kendra, with all her strengths, must allow it to "come home" by submitting to it instead of trying to attain it.

Message: Obtaining wisdom in love is possible when you remain open to universal forces. With a humble attitude, allow yourself to honor the unexplainable power of love.

Love Powers

	♡ EVA	□ KENDRA	○ NIXA	▫ BELINDA	☽ DIANA	△ ERIKA
○ NIXA #1 GUIDE	○♡	○□	○○	○▫	○☽	○△

○ ♡ Nixa/Eva

Nixa and Eva both fly high when it comes to love. Both of them enjoy being catered to and wined and dined by men, and neither of them is a homebody. They yearn for excitement and interesting experiences. Eva encourages Nixa to flirt outrageously and, in general, throw everything she's got into her romance. For her part, Nixa doesn't have any problems with that as long as it doesn't take away from her first love: artistic endeavors or creative work.

Eva shows Nixa how to be a little more relaxed about her love life. If Nixa isn't presently involved with a man, she may need to take the time to find someone who is compatible. Similarly, if she's in a relationship, it may be necessary for Nixa to integrate her love life into her creative life so that its demands don't feel like a constant interruption. Since Nixa has a positive, flexible attitude, Eva can easily make headway when she talks about love. Nixa is friendly, charming, and original. She's open to bonding with a man, but only on her terms. Eva brings a bit of tolerance into the picture.

Nixa easily picks up on the concept of a warm, generous love affair, however, she often finds it hard to follow through when it comes to giving. Selfishness and self-centeredness surface in situations where Nixa wants to be a superstar. With Eva's guidance, she can get in touch with her own feelings about reciprocity. At times, Nixa loses track of what she can offer her love relationship. Here Eva can help Nixa explore the possibilities.

Message: Mutual care and concern between lovers counteracts the tension of everyday demands. Tolerance and an unselfish attitude open the door to enormous possibilities for love.

○ □ Nixa/Kendra

Nixa is a creative free spirit who realizes that a relationship often needs change to keep it alive. She's quick, sensitive, and aware of her partner's innermost needs—and she's into what's most fun to do together. But she tends to love her own mind's creation of her lover rather than the real-life man who may, at times, be a bit boring or intimidating. Kendra helps Nixa cut through the illusions. Her objectivity allows Nixa to come a little closer to seeing the relationship as it really is.

Nixa has a tendency to go too far as a free spirit, and when she does, she can become love's victim. If she flies too high, she will be hurt—but if she comes too far down to earth, she could be crushed. Kendra is there to help Nixa temper her free-wheeling notions with a small amount of clearheaded awareness.

Buoyant, optimistic, and playful by nature, Nixa's needs in love matters are varied and uninhibited. She's not one to be concerned with duties or practical matters. It's not often that she needs Kendra's advice about relationships. Men, to her, are a wonderful, almost mythical experience that she doesn't want to ground. But she realizes that she needs Kendra's help to cut through romantic misconceptions at the beginning of a relationship. She's smart enough to know that love at first sight doesn't necessarily lead to true love. But she needs Kendra to help her think more clearly and to ask her some important questions about real possibilities for love.

Message: Cutting through romantic illusions about love is necessary at the beginning of a relationship. Before becoming deeply involved, explore your feelings in a levelheaded way. It is necessary to find the delicate balance between heart and mind—and to act out of that centeredness.

○ ○ Nixa/Nixa

When Nixa relies only on herself in love matters, she can become idealistic and overly romantic. The image of her beloved can be imaginatively made-up of whole cloth, and very often it's unrelated to the real-life partner with whom she has to confront everyday problems. Nixa needs the calm centeredness of a Helping Guide who can help her understand the true nature of love. To become grounded, she needs guidance in interpreting her feelings and experiences—and a balanced point of view.

○ ʊ Nixa/Belinda

The Nixa/Belinda combination can be a push-me, pull-you affair. In matters of the heart, Belinda can be naïve and trusting. She is happy and wholesome, and she usually lets the man take the lead in sex. Nixa, on the other hand, is street smart and sophisticated. She can be a bit strange, bizarre, or kinky, and she asserts herself sexually or surrenders to men depending on the whim of the moment.

Despite their differences, Belinda can help Nixa put her resources into combining home life and creative endeavors. With Belinda's guidance, Nixa can balance the regular timetable of domesticity with the flexibility of creative time. If Nixa has children now (or wants to have them in the future), Belinda can offer the structure of family life—although it is up to Nixa to integrate that into her own urges and compulsiveness to create.

Nixa likes being in love, but she doesn't cherish the thought of responsibility. Playfulness, affectionate words and gestures, and spontaneous lovemaking are expressions of love. Since she doesn't want to be bogged down by commitments, Nixa very often discounts Belinda's concerned advice. But Nixa does listen to Belinda when the decisions of marriage or having a baby come up.

Message: In love partnerships, imagination, spontaneity, and style can promote growth. When family life is a concern between two people, harmony between the productive-creative self and domestic responsibilities can be achieved by grounding energy in the home.

○ ☽ Nixa/Diana

Watch out for this Guide pair. It can bring negative results on the love front. Nixa with her creative ways and Diana with her strong feelings about solitude can pull each other away from a solid relationship. Both are strong! And together they can easily go their merry way instead of directing their love powers.

Nixa can be mercurial when she's crossed by her lover; she may misread Diana's guidance and go off alone to angrily sit it out instead of creatively exploring her feelings. Stressful love situations are when Nixa needs Diana most. She needs the insight and newfound assurance that comes from contemplating her experiences.

On the other hand, when Nixa is in a happy, healthy relationship—one that allows her the freedom to be imaginative and playful without being put down or curtailed—she is attentive to devoting quiet moments to reflection. Whether Nixa's relationship or marriage is happy or unhappy, with Diana's guidance, she will spend some time alone to form a more solid, independent self.

Message: The heart has its reasons—and watchfulness and mindfulness are necessary to know them in all their aspects. Take time, not to count the reasons, but to meditate on them creatively.

○ △ Nixa/Erika

Erika has an uncanny ability to see into the future. This is what appeals to Nixa when she consults Erika. Nixa wants to experience change in a positive way, and she wants to see her future love life progressing romantically. An enduring, loveless relationship is definitely not for Nixa. If Erika sagely tells her that her love affair is at a standstill or is coming to an impasse, Nixa's first response is to deny it. Erika then provides Nixa with the capacity to handle her sometimes screwball dreams in a way that promotes growth instead of leading to a dead end. Nixa is a dreamer, and Erika can help make her dreams a reality, while at the same time discarding wacky notions and whimsical caprices that only stand in the way of true intimacy.

Nixa doesn't give up her beguiling fantasies easily, but Erika is strong and powerful in presenting her case. When Nixa overdoes it and molds her man into what she wants instead of seeing him for who he is, it's time to let go of overly romantic projections. Since Nixa doesn't always see this herself, it is up to Erika to point it out.

When this Guide pair are working together, they allow balance to be created between ideal love and real love.

Message: Without effort, harmony is created when dream and actuality converge. Like two waters that make one tide, love unites and flows.

	♡ EVA	□ KENDRA	○ NIXA	◘ BELINDA	☽ DIANA	△ ERIKA
◘ BELINDA #1 GUIDE	◘ ♡	◘ □	◘ ○	◘ ◘	◘ ☽	◘ △

◘ ♡ Belinda/Eva

Belinda usually maintains a steady state when it comes to love relationships. Sex tends to be fairly predictable, and Belinda usually doesn't have strong erotic feelings. Belinda is sensitive and romantic, and she's patient with a lover whose sexual responses are temporarily limited. The basic formula for Belinda's love life is gentle sex combined with sentimental words and affectionate gestures: When she wants to learn to express her love in more subtle ways, she calls upon Eva.

Strong physical desire is not a part of Belinda's nature, but she is quick to reach out for love. An ideal mate and sexual compatibility are important to her. When her own sexual and emotional responses to her partner are dulled, she can turn to Eva for guidance. For Belinda, the air must be cleared and the issues that are preventing sexual fulfillment explored.

Belinda can be extremely turned off by intense, explosive lovemaking. She finds it difficult to adjust to extreme sexual differences between herself and her partner. Eva can present solutions to this and other problems relating to sexual harmony.

Eva can go overboard in expressing the need for total sensuality. But Belinda is smart, and she can wisely pick what she needs for her situation. Belinda insists on being loved for who she is, and not only for her attractiveness. Eva can guide her just so far, then her own capacities for love must take over.

Message: Harmony results from embracing new, subtle ways of lovemaking and ironing out present incompatibilities.

⊡ ☐ Belinda/Kendra

In a love relationship, Belinda is nourishing, protective, and devoted. She wants closeness and commitment from a partner. And she wants her partner to recognize how important "nesting" and being part of a family is to her. Belinda's main emotional bonds are made in the home.

Sex, for her, is a joyful way of expressing her devotion, and she wants that devotion recognized and returned by her partner. A strong sense of relatedness is necessary for her sexual fulfillment, and she expects her man to take the lead in sex. A sense of real partnership and intimacy—and a shared life together—go hand in hand with lovemaking.

Kendra, as her Helping Guide, will help Belinda to expand her vision. While the home will always be Belinda's base, Kendra will subtly communicate the rewards of other kinds of journeys—a career, travel, friendships, sports, etc. Kendra shows Belinda how journeying away from hearth and home can enrich love and sexuality. With Kendra's help, Belinda can become more of a "doer" in the outside world, and she can bring a very special assertive femininity into lovemaking.

Belinda can be very active and assertive within the confines of her protected environment. She can get things done—hiring carpenters, electricians, scheduling PTA meetings, etc. In her negative aspect, she will enlist Kendra's actualizing "get the job done" power only within her closed circle. It is Belinda's task to awaken and become conscious of the outer world of opinion, ideas, and differing visions of life. Kendra will help Belinda become aware of the broad range of emotions that exist outside the home and become receptive to new feelings about love within herself. Bringing this particular kind of receptivity into her love relationship will enrich and enliven it.

Message: Assertiveness in lovemaking and receptivity to new emotions about love can be enhanced by expanding your horizons.

☉ ○ Belinda/Nixa

Belinda relies on Nixa to help her put some adventure into her love life. When romance becomes boring, Nixa can show Belinda how to put some renewed passion into an intimate relationship. Nixa's greater spontaneity can also get Belinda thinking along totally new and original lines. When Belinda drops her guard a bit, she will find sex will be less inhibited and more fulfilling.

To Belinda, security is important in her love relationship. With Nixa as her Guide, she can learn to trust her feelings and to express them to her lover. This newfound self-assurance provides her with the stability she needs—and she can then go out from that center to explore the many new directions love can take.

Nixa sees Belinda through the changes in her love relationship. Belinda is usually determined to make things work despite emotional outbursts or financial disagreements. Here's where Nixa can help Belinda with plans that offer imaginative solutions. Belinda is devoted and dutiful, and with Nixa's help she can bring a sense of freedom into her relationship and then make effortless contributions to it.

Message: Renewing love's passion takes imagination. Freedom from inhibition and effortless movement toward trusting and expressing your feelings are necessary first steps.

☉ ☉ Belinda/Belinda

Belinda is her own Helping Guide here, and in some instances this Guide pair can be a very creative force for maintaining balance. When Belinda is true to her own nature, she forms and enjoys a love relationship that is centered in the home. She's not caught up in the trendiness of being a superwoman, and she doesn't have to apologize for her priorities. Belinda is committed to preserving her personal identity, while at the same time seeing herself as part of a couple. A professional identity is not something she strives for.

The Belinda/Belinda combination often works well in relationships where the man is appreciative and caring. If Belinda's lover or husband is offhand or unaffectionate, Belinda may feel insecure and uncertain about her own needs and values.

When Belinda maintains a strong connection to the world outside the home, balance in the love relationship can be maintained. If Belinda is self-absorbed and narrow in her perspective, the love relationship will suffer and become limited and stifling to both partners.

☋ ☽ Belinda/Diana

Diana can guide Belinda to be more independent in love matters. Belinda tends to minimize her lover's faults and make the most of his virtues. She's supportive, but her care and concern are very often taken for granted. When all the attention is on her man and Belinda takes more and more responsibility for defining the relationship and giving it direction, things get off kilter and become skewed. It's at this point that Belinda becomes resentful and frustrated. With Diana's guidance, Belinda can find out how to change things around so that she can enjoy her relationship more instead of trying to mother it. Belinda has to understand that she too can be in the limelight part of the time, and that she doesn't have to take total responsibility for determining how the relationship is going to grow.

Diana's independent frame of mind can influence Belinda to ask her partner for emotional support when she needs it. Diana insists on being cared for as an autonomous individual, and this is the guidance she gives Belinda. Since Belinda tends to be dependent on her man, it's sometimes difficult for her to think of herself as a separate, self-actualizing person instead of part of a couple.

Diana also advises Belinda to be sexually honest with her lover and ask for what she needs in order to be fulfilled. Belinda's emphasis is on satisfying her partner. With Diana's guidance, she can become more aware of her own desires and assert them without hesitation, embarrassment, or fear.

Message: Independence and autonomy in a relationship promote growth of the individual and the relationship.

◻ △ Belinda/Erika

Belinda is patient and considerate, but when her partner ignores her or is abusive, she has a tendency to withdraw. Emotional involvements that drain Belinda's resources can be frightening and debilitating. Loss of self-esteem and self-confidence are the result. Belinda knows that Erika's guidance will help to solve the problem in a way that forces her to face the real issues.

If children are involved, Belinda needs Erika's help even more. In reconciling turbulent situations, Erika takes a calm approach, trying always to bring things together instead of splitting them apart. With her age-old wisdom, Erika can show Belinda how to remember the healing power of love. On a practical side, Belinda can learn how to state her position without attacking her partner. She can also find out how to listen with her heart, while at the same time striving for a resolution that incorporates care and concern for herself.

Outward agreement between partners doesn't necessarily mean the issues have been resolved. Erika understands and advises Belinda that inner work must be done. Guilt, vindictiveness, and anger all have to be released before forgiveness can occur. The greater task of beginning anew can then be addressed.

Message: Relationships in trouble must start with the healing heart—and then move in a practical way toward solving specific problems. Agreement, forgiveness, and starting afresh are necessary for wounds to heal and renewal to take place.

	♡ EVA	◻ KENDRA	○ NIXA	◻ BELINDA	☽ DIANA	△ ERIKA
☽ DIANA #1 GUIDE	☽♡	☽ ◻	☽○	☽ ◻	☽☽	☽△

☽ ♡ Diana/Eva

Diana is self-reliant and she promotes self-discovery. Her original thinking calls for sustained use of the imagination, and a degree of solitude is virtually essential. At times she finds it difficult to make satisfactory intimate attachments. Eva sympathizes with Diana's need for privacy, but she is also ready to bring her into the world of interpersonal relationships and help her find true happiness.

Diana fully realizes the importance of having a man in her life, but her primary concentration is not on her love life. Her relationship is a hub on which her life revolves, but not the main one. Eva guides Diana so that solitude becomes less idealized in her mind and is balanced with the capacity to form an equal and lasting relationship with a partner.

Determination is a strong Diana characteristic, and so is stubbornness. Through gentle persuasion, Eva can help her learn to appreciate and value her own sensuality. Diana often finds that rejection puts a damper on erotic enthusiasm. Here Eva can help her resolve the issue by encouraging her to think it through. Diana daydreams of a lover who is her best friend, and Eva guides her in gradually transforming her relationship, regardless of how reciprocal Diana believes her partner's efforts to be.

In general, Eva helps Diana in joining with a partner in genuine love. She shows Diana how communication, consideration, and camaraderie can exist alongside a desire for privacy. With Eva's guidance, Diana can keep her solitary ways and at the same time form a strong attachment to her lover.

Message: A need for privacy and the growth of a relationship are dualities that need not be in opposition. Solitude and commitment to a partner offer different opportunities for genuine love to prosper.

☽ ☐ Diana/Kendra

This combination can often oppose each other, but when they click, they can be very powerful. Diana needs solitude, and when she has Kendra as a Helping Guide for work, she can accomplish a great deal. When she has Kendra as a Helping Guide for love, she can take time out to sift and sort and refine her experience of love. Solitude is as necessary for love to grow as togetherness is. When Diana is with a partner, she can be touched and moved; she can care, appreciate, and wonder. It is only when she is alone, however, that she can expand her capacity for love. Kendra helps Diana find, in solitude, her own center, her source of harmony and beneficence. Kendra can teach Diana the rewards of returning to her relationship from a place of solitude with more insight, refined energy, and a conviction to achieve harmony. The way of Kendra is dedication and courage. The advice she gives to Diana is that love grows through contemplation and action in the world.

Sex is not of utmost importance to Diana. What is important to her is that she is able to maintain her separate self—a self that is in harmony with the needs and desires of her partner. Balance is the key here, and Diana looks to Kendra to help achieve it.

The danger for Diana is that she may spend *too* much time in solitude, away from the relationship instead of nurturing it. Instead of putting her trust in the relationship, she may spend too much time analyzing it, or too much time trying to get away from issues she doesn't want to confront and deal with. Or she may prefer solitude to the relationship itself. By listening only to her own strong need for solitude, she can shut Kendra out, when what is called for is attention to her personal relationships.

Message: Solitude can promote insight and expand the capacity to love. Contemplation combined with positive action is a basic way of the feminine.

☽ ○ Diana/Nixa

Nixa brings versatility, mental alertness, and quickness of perception into Diana's self-reliant life. Both Diana and Nixa are strong individuals, each with their own vision of life. Neither one is oversensitive or emotionally aware—and neither is practical. Nixa tends to be impulsive and spontaneous about love, whereas Diana can be rigid and sometimes snobbish. It is here that Nixa can be the most help, pulling Diana out of her own timid rules into the wider world of romantic involvement.

Both Diana and Nixa are concerned about being generous with

their time. Self-discovery, creative pursuits, and solitude are often more important to them than happiness in a relationship.

Nixa's inventiveness helps Diana realize that togetherness in a relationship is most valuable where there is common ground. When Diana and her partner share activities they both love, the relationship is strengthened. Time spent on distractions or idle activities saps them both of vitality. Chores and everyday maintenance aside, Diana can be accommodating about setting aside time with her partner when she knows it will be rewarding. Nixa is there to give her direction and encouragment.

If true love has eluded Diana up to now, Nixa can counsel her to come out of her cocoon. Diana has many wrongheaded perceptions about how her partner should look and be—so much so that she may even crush the enjoyment or the potential for love out of present relationships. The ideas Diana has of what it would take to make love possible are often erroneous. Nixa wisely advises Diana to seek out what is ordinary in a partner, as well as what is special.

Message: Love cannot be predetermined by setting up conditions or requirements for a perfect mate. Nor will togetherness be furthered unless generous time is allotted for rewarding activities.

☽ ☌ Diana/Belinda

Belinda can help Diana establish a connection to home and family. In her positive aspects, Diana is self-assured and confident about her independence and her need for solitude. In her negative aspects, she can become dismissive of her relationship and contemptuous of her partner. A self-righteous, haughty attitude prevails during these times, and false pride can keep her from reestablishing loving contact with her man. Belinda's all-embracing care and nurturing qualities show Diana how to come out of her self-imposed emotional isolation and become more attached to an environment that encourages love.

Belinda's strong ties to her man are romantic and practical. She is touchingly affectionate and in tender words and gestures she's mindful of the small everyday things that animate a wholesome relationship. And these are attitudes she conveys to Diana. While maintaining independence, Diana can, at the same time, keep an open channel to the nurturing part of herself. Belinda helps her appreciate that her independent stance can be tempered by warmth and loyalty to the relationship. Diana realizes that she lacks devotion. To go from her own self-absorbed world into an atmosphere that can sustain lasting love, she needs Belinda's help.

Diana is not the mothering sort, but she can be thoughtful, caring, and cheerful. With Belinda's guidance, Diana can learn to express tenderness toward her lover. Without being obstinate, Diana can reflect on the mood and surroundings she has created to attract love.

Message: When love's setting becomes tender, optimistic, and caring, the relationship can progress in positive ways. Solitary reflection begins the process of devotion.

☽ ☽ Diana/Diana

Diana with only herself as a Helping Guide can create powerful negative forces that pull her away from love. A very strong, independent, and self-reliant nature makes Diana highly opinionated and inflexible at times. Like a supple young tree, she must bend with the wind as it blows. To find love or to rekindle the flames, Diana needs a Helping Guide who will teach her different ways of leaving her present isolated position. If love has eluded Diana up to now, it is because she hasn't allowed herself to rely on wisdom other than her own. Diana can profit immensely by finding a Helping Guide who can balance her deepest desires with her needs for solitude.

☽ △ Diana/Erika

Erika understands Diana's strengths and weaknesses in love matters. Mutual consideration between partners is necessary, and when

Diana is in a relationship but has one foot out the door, Erika shows her how to strengthen her relationship by being more centered in it. Diana can then give her love life the time and space it needs to thrive.

If Diana wants to have children eventually, Erika will help her create a strong bond of trust with her partner, so that the path to motherhood becomes easier as time passes. While Diana will always be an independent lover, Erika can guide Diana toward understanding her own needs for emotional fulfillment. Diana is stable and dependable, but she can descend into selfishness, rigidity, depression, and loneliness. Erika is there to help prevent Diana from becoming too isolated. And she can draw Diana into the wider world of close affection and love.

Erika's discrimination, patience, and strength of purpose combine to make the most of Diana's optimism and candor. She shows Diana how to accentuate the positive aspects of her relationship — and how to use her meditative time to work on issues that are troublesome.

Diana is well aware that her solitary ways are absolutely necessary, but she also realizes that give-and-take with a lover will bring her the wholeness she desires.

Message: Peace of mind is achieved when a solitary nature and a loving nature are reconciled within.

	♡ EVA	□ KENDRA	○ NIXA	◘ BELINDA	☽ DIANA	△ ERIKA
△ ERIKA #1 GUIDE	△ ♡	△ □	△ ○	△ ◘	△ ☽	△ △

△ ♡ Erika/Eva

Erika understands women's mysteries in a deeply profound way. She has spiritual awareness, philosophical insight, and psychic understanding. But when it comes to love, Erika needs Eva for down-to-earth practicality. Erika needs to, at times, leave the stratosphere for her high-minded perceptions and experience more of the joys of sensual pleasure. Erika usually picks a partner whose level of awareness and sensitivity is as high as her own. If he is also sexually interesting, so much the better.

Erika has enormous capacity for love, but she's cautious about verbal or physical commitment. She takes her time deciding, but when she does, Erika's fidelity is enduring. Sexual compatibility may take a while in her relationship. It is here that Eva can help Erika to be honest in sharing her emotions with her partner. Service to others is an important part of Erika's life, so in trying to please her man, she can lose sight of her own feelings or withhold them.

With Eva's guidance, Erika can bring openness and sincerity into her love life. When Erika overcomes some of her timidity, she can be a little more daring about letting her lover know her needs and desires.

Message: Honesty and straightforwardness always make a solid base for compatibility.

△ □ Erika/Kendra

Erika, as the wise woman, understands feminine secrets in a profound way. She wants to bring her awareness of love's mysteries into her relationship. But doing this in a timely way that strengthens rather than weakens the romantic relationship isn't always easy for Erika. It is Kendra's single-mindedness and determination that will help Erika tell her partner the things that mean the most to her. That means talking about her feelings, showing her vulnerability, and giving affection to her partner, while at the same time realizing that her man's experience of love, although it has a caring dimension, is very different from hers.

Erika has a difficult task. She must talk to her partner from her deepest feminine self, with the knowledge that he may not understand all—or, in fact, any—of what she is saying. Erika acts out of an active, feeling center that is intuitive. While her man is practical and caring, he is often not terribly emotionally sensitive. Kendra's perseverance is necessary here, as is her dedication to helping Erika create an interdependent relationship with her man, one that can balance her awareness and attentiveness with his more practical care and thoughtfulness.

Message: When lovers do not share the same understanding about love, symmetry can be achieved by mutual discovery. Genuine, lasting love requires more than one definition of happiness.

△ ○ Erika/Nixa

The Erika/Nixa combination is a strong one—and in matters of the heart it can be very powerful. When they are balanced, Erika's wise perceptions and Nixa's inventiveness can attract true love. Erika is grounded in tranquility, and Nixa flies high on spontaneity. When they work together harmoniously, Erika can create the warm, devoted relationship she wants with her lover.

Erika learns the value of change from Nixa. When old, tired ways of being in a relationship are discarded and new, open, and flexible ways take their place—pessimism, selfishness, obstinacy, and self-deception melt away. Nixa shows Erika how to make decisions in ways that are not hackneyed. Nixa is an original thinker, and while she may not always be especially aware of her emotions, she brings Erika new and innovative ideas for positive change and growth in a relationship.

With Erika's intuitive sense and Nixa's creativity, there is room for a broad range of possibilities in Erika's love life. Her social life can become more varied and interesting, and she can look for new ways to change to encourage emotional closeness.

Message: When worn-out attitudes are discarded, it is possible to become attached to new, innovative ideas and heartfelt feelings. Trust that a true union with your beloved can occur by sharing new attitudes.

△ ʊ Erika/Belinda

Belinda is always looking for ways to enjoy routine togetherness with her man. Everyday experiences—cooking and at-home entertaining, sports or family activities, and just hanging out together—

are opportunities that can favor emotional closeness. Belinda encourages Erika to take an affirmative approach to love—one that includes a wedding and babies.

Rather than struggling to open communication, initiating discussions about intimacy, or trying to solve problems, Belinda believes that mutual discovery between lovers can be achieved in ordinary moments. Erika wants her partner and herself to bring out the best in each other, and Belinda show her how this is possible through common, everyday experiences. Belinda also teaches Erika to appreciate domesticity as a foundation for love. Belinda believes in long-term unions and in integrating romantic love into a functional life. Her simplicity and trustfulness help Erika drop her rigid defenses and break her own rules for love. Belinda insists on respectful affection, and with her guidance, Erika can look within to see if her own values need to be changed.

Message: Ordinary shared experiences between lovers can often bring true intimacy. Look past stale, conventional attitudes to find real love existing in the commonplace.

△ ☽ Erika/Diana

In love matters, Erika is wise and powerful. Diana gives her the necessary strength and independence to pull away from her love relationship every once in a while. When what is needed is a fresh look at how and where the relationship is going, Diana provides the necessary dispassionate attitude. At the beginning of a relationship, Diana can be especially helpful in insisting that Erika take some quiet time away from her partner to look at how this new man is or is not meeting her needs—and at how and what Erika is giving to herself, to her lover, to the relationship.

A lot of time isn't necessary here. But some contemplative moments do release new awareness of what's going on in a love relationship. Since Diana can sometimes be skittish about men, Erika has to be careful about listening to her advice. She also has to be mindful about living her love relationships instead of thinking about them too much. Erika does best in relationships with men who have a large vocabulary for their emotions and who are sophisticated in understanding their inner drives. Erika is often attracted to men in positions of power.

Diana, on the other hand, is attracted to men who are low-key, nonthreatening, and unemotional.

When Erika relies too much on Diana's perceptions about men, she feels conflicted. It is best for Erika to limit Diana's guidance to helping her establish solitary watchfulness. During these times, Erika can find out more about what she wants to give and get from her love relationship.

Message: Watchfulness and mindfulness are necessary in any love relationship. In quiet moments, a dispassionate attitude can provide insight into the bonds between two partners.

△ △ Erika/Erika

Erika can be a very powerful force in attracting love and keeping it alive. With only herself as a Helping Guide, she is almost assured of finding happiness. Occasionally, she does not have the kind of guidance that another viewpoint provides. But her energy is positive, and she won't hesitate to seek help when she needs it. Erika's deep wisdom combines with itself and doubles when she is her own Helping Guide. In matters of the heart, the results are almost always positive.

Releasing Love Powers means transforming messages into practical, workable energy. When you receive messages with your heart and pay mindful attention to them, you automatically release the power of love. It is up to you to use this energy in everyday experiences and situations.

To give an example of how this can be done, let's suppose that your Guide pair △ ♡ Erika/Eva has given you the message: "Honesty and straightforwardness always make a solid base for compatibility."

Reflect on the message by asking yourself three questions:

How does this speak to my situation as it exists at this time?

What has to happen for positive change to occur?

How will my life be different after the relationship is transformed?

Messages Speak to Your Condition

When Quakers say, "It speaks to my condition," they mean that whatever has been said hits home. It rings a bell; it strikes the right note. Something within can respond deeply to a message that corresponds exactly to an issue you have been recently thinking about or working on. Or the message can relate to a state of mind. If you've been depressed or lonely, a few words can snap you out of the doldrums when you *respond* to them.

Acknowledging that the words are a key factor to seeing the light enables you to appreciate the messages even more.

Going back to the △ ♡ Erika/Eva example above, some questions you could ask yourself are:

What are the issues surrounding honesty in my present relationship?

Has candor been a problem before?

How important to me is honesty in a relationship?

In general, what you are doing is finding out how the messages tie in with your situation as it exists today.

Messages Allow Positive Change to Take Place

You—and you alone—know exactly what inner work and outer action has to take place for positive change to take place. The message merely points the way. In the △ ♡ Erika/Eva example, you could ask yourself such questions as:

Is there a way I can be more open with myself? With my lover?

Are there obstructions on the path to total honesty?

What are my secret fears? My hopes?

Do doubts about my own integrity stand in the way of future plans?

Am I in the dark about what kind of honesty I want?

What are the small steps I have to take? How about a giant one?

Basically, you are realizing exactly how the message can be used to take action for positive change.

Messages Transform the Relationship

Once you realize how the message speaks to your situation as it is now, and you understand what action has to be taken for positive change to occur, you can begin to ask yourself how your life will be different after the relationship is transformed.

In the △ ♡ Erika/Eva example, here are some questions that can clarify just how life will be different:

What positive benefits can I expect from a more candid relationship?

Are there any negative aspects that have to be circumvented?

How can I guard against slipping back into insincere habits?

When my wishes for honesty are attained, how will my relationship be altered?

Here you are beginning to understand the rewards of positive change.

Releasing Love Powers

When you accept messages with your heart and ask questions with mindful attention to the answers, you can begin to bring your newfound realizations into everyday life. By now you have enough confidence in your own self-knowledge to put your faith into practice.

If you have faith in your own power to love, it will be released. In the △ ♡ Erika/Eva example, the message "Honesty and straightforwardness always make a solid base for compatibility" is just an idle truism unless you direct energy into specific areas of your life. The message has to be *lived* to become alive. Otherwise, the energy for releasing Love Powers remains inert.

Change in Motion

Change is in motion. After you complete working on the message from your Guide pair, you can (in your own time), continue by combining your #1 Guide with each of the other five Helping Guides. Begin with a combination of your choice and work with this Guide pair until completion. As you did before, read the message, ask yourself the three questions (and other necessary questions), and begin to release Love Powers by actualizing the love energy in daily life.

Before working with the next Guide pair, it is in your best interest to complete work with the previous Guide pair. To complete work with your Guide pair means that you have released Love Powers and you have been able to make some positive changes in your everyday life.

Proceed at your own pace. Remember, there is no need to rush.

If you arrive at a standstill or obstruction, do not be discouraged. You can return at another time to whatever now seems unclear or irrelevant. Continue now with another Guide pair and work with that message.

Again, remember that your #1 Guide changes during different life phases. In this chapter, you have all the material you need to work with all the different combinations of Guide pairs.

part

2

The words for feminine in the synonym finder are: soft, delicate, gentle, tender, docile, submissive, amenable, deferential. To that we are adding powerful, strong, fearless, energetic, courageous.

The quest for Inner Feminine Power requires that you *allow* yourself these attributes. The journey toward Inner Feminine Unity is a path on which you *use* these qualities every single day.

In Part Two, you will relearn to trust your intuition, compassion, love, and devotion . . . and to trust the trust you inherently feel. These are all attributes you were born with. They are your heritage and your birthright. You are entitled to use them to empower you. Entitlement, empowerment, and envisionment. As a self-actualizing woman it is up to you to envision your own past, present, and future in a productive way.

This book was designed to reacquaint you with the full,

deep experience of your own womanhood. It was written to connect you with the secrets of your power, strength, fearlessness, and courage. Feminine attributes were given you as a great gift. Rather than repressing them, it is time to rediscover them, to use them creatively in your everyday life.

In today's world the feminine qualities of intuition, compassion, love, devotion, receptivity, and trust have been put out to pasture. We're taught to value what's "more important": rational, linear, verbal thinking.

Not only have we devalued these feminine qualities, we've been taught to repress them so that eventually we see them as evil. It is at this point that we women give ourselves inner taboos so that we can deal with this perceived "evil" by avoiding it.

This inner degradation of feminine qualities leads to self-rejection and gives us an *inner* image of inferiority and a sense of self-hate.

It may seem strange to think of love or compassion as something we've devalued, but in fact, as these qualities become more and more narrowly defined by our culture, the expression of true devotion or real intimacy is actually being severely curtailed.

Part Two of the book will explore these feminine qualities and allow each individual woman to discover and learn to be guided by her *own experience* of intuition, compassion, love, devotion, receptivity, and trust. Women are mostly unaware of the true nature and power of these qualities—and therefore they're prevented from experiencing them as fully as they can as a source of empowerment. Each of these qualities is an *intelligence* that may, at present, be undeveloped or repressed. In Part Two you will learn to awaken this intelligence and use it in your best interests in day-to-day situations.

The end of the book will wrap up what you have learned, but for you it will be just a beginning. It will be the start of your own transformation. You will convert what you now know about yourself and your Inner Feminine Power into major inner breakthroughs and prosperity. (Remember that whatever happens on the inner plane is reflected in the outer world. When the inner work that you do on yourself is recognized and used creatively in daily life, the transformative process is at work.) Major inner achievements occur when you receive and accept your Inner Feminine Power — and when you let go of your refusal to let it flow through you.

Prosperity occurs when you bring your knowledge into the everyday world and *use* it. There is a story about a rabbit who went to the mountain top with other rabbits to become enlightened. The rabbit stayed there for many years and gained great self-knowledge. At last she realized that the trick was not to stay up on the mountain with other rabbits, but to come down into the valley and live with jackals. Only in the challenge of *using* self-knowledge will you prosper!

Inner Feminine Power is now available to you. In the final chapters you will learn how to get it going, and you'll find out how to create and bring Inner Feminine Unity into your everyday life.

In your own time, begin Part Two with the feeling that there is a unifying force within that can bring all the disparate parts of yourself together in new ways.

Feel the energy for transformation and unity flow through you. Try and stay with that energy as you read the second half of this book.

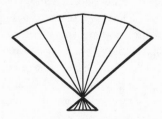

Inner Feminine Power is your vital life force. It's your boundless *aliveness*, your essence of being. You can call it zing, bounce, zest, verve, snap, vitality, ardor, exuberance—anything you want. It's an energy you exude, and at the same time a force within that you can tap. Inner Feminine Power is always available to you. When you reach within for it and release it into the outer world in a continuous flow, it becomes as natural as breathing.

A characteristic of the positive dynamic and transformative Inner Feminine Power is that it is active and liberating. It can be used to effect change, extend limits, generate passion and lead to healthy emotional involvements. It opens the heart and mind to enjoyment and risk taking, and it inspires and expects positive change to occur.

When you are using full Inner Feminine Power, you are in the First Space—a place where you are trustful, intuitive, compassionate, loving, and receptive. You are optimistic, concerned, and protective. With full power you feel secure, accepted, hopeful, and giving.

When you are filled with fears and doubts, your ability to tap and release your Inner Feminine Power diminishes. When tension and anxiety, envy, or greed and anger prevent or limit a continuous flow of energy, you are in the Second Space—a place where resentment, confusion, and helplessness reign. It's a place where you can easily disregard others and sever relationships. Acting aggressively, rejecting and depriving others, becoming addicted to your own negative thought processes, and being possessive are some of the limiting behaviors in the Second Space. Depression is a common emotional response, and indecisiveness is its behavioristic counterpart.

To help keep the energy flowing toward the positive First Space and away from the negative Second Space, it is sometimes necessary to go to the Third Space. This is a place of new possibilities. In the Third Space, new channels to your Inner Feminine are created, new motivations and hopes, new boundaries and limits, and new self-images are born. The Third Space is a place of renewal. It is a vantage point from which you can look at your situation and experience in an entirely new way, where you can observe yourself in a nonjudgmental, rational way.

The Third Space is a birthing room, a hatching place, an incubation space for ideas, thoughts, feelings. It's not a place where you have to *do* anything. You only need open your heart, witness your responses, and *feel* your energy flowing in an affirmative direction. Every time you incubate, hatch, ponder, meditate, muse, reflect, contemplate, and consider your life from a new perspective, you are in the Third Space.

Whenever you are coming from the Second Space, you're limiting the energy flow. When you come from the First Space, the energy flows creatively and continuously without your having to think about it. And whenever you come from the Third Space, you have the possibility of integrating new energies into your experience and using them in everyday life, for yourself and for others.

Many self-development books for women are filled with concepts that describe the reader as a woman-warrior-heroine on a journey toward self-fulfillment, or as a goddess who can learn how to cope from other goddesses. As we go into the twenty-first century, we need new models, new self-images, and new inspiration. Working toward your own positive self-growth is not enough. It is necessary to reach out and touch and enrich the lives of others. Full Inner Feminine Power can flow freely only when you are motivated by the heart that can feel and express love.

Attributes of the Heart

In the following chapters, you will learn to use the *intelligence* of intuition, love, compassion, devotion, trust, and receptivity. They all come from the brilliance of the heart and can be acted on later by the discipline of the mind. We call them "attributes of the heart."

Entering the Third Space requires that you take a leap. You won't find what you are looking for unless you go beyond the boundaries of your usual understanding. Conventional thinking treats subjects like intuition as "emotional" and somehow a distraction from reality. In the Third Space, intuition (as well as the other attributes of the heart) is regarded as a form of intelligence that is different from rational thinking, but nonetheless just as real.

To a certain degree, everyone has intuition, love, compassion,

Venus Unbound

devotion, trust, and receptivity. In the Third Space you will return to what you already know, strengthen it, and use it differently. To do this, it is necessary to go beyond what is comprehensible to the rational mind. In the Third Space, the attributes of the heart may even conflict with reason. Almost everybody can understand that love knows things absolutely and doesn't need a rational explanation. When you're in love you communicate with your lover and reach conclusions about him and the relationship through a process that has nothing to do with objective measurement. And when you think about your life as a totality, there are many other intelligent actions that rely on information that remains incomprehensible to the mind.

Let's take a moment to focus on what the Third Space is. It is a room for the inexplicable. It is a place of silent awakening to what is alive within. In the Third Space, you will find what you need—which is not necessarily what you think you need—to express your aliveness. Instead of reasonableness, goal setting, and striving for perfection and completion, you will witness your innate intelligence and experience who you are in a new way.

The following exercise will help you enter the Third Space—the place of new possibilities—in a way that brings you closer to what is alive within.

Stand up and close your eyes. Relax your body. Picture yourself in the center of a small circle. This is the center of the world. There are no bits or parts or pieces or fragments—there is only a whole you and a small circle surrounding and protecting you.

The center is a place where new possibilities enfold. Begin to feel how alive you are inside the circle. Feel what is important to you. Let images and thoughts surface, and observe them as if you are looking at clouds. (Pause.) Witness them and let them pass. (Pause.)

Remain in the center of what is alive for you. Without interfering in your feelings, thoughts, and sensations, experience what is unfolding. (Pause for about two minutes.)

Stay with whatever is alive within and return to your usual waking reality. Open your eyes and stretch your body.

In the Third Space, you remember and release what you already know. The attributes of the heart are also memories of the truth that can be released in the Third Space. Before taking a look at intuition, love, compassion, devotion, trust and receptivity, here are five basic rules to observe while you are in the Third Space:

1. *Learn to trust your responses.* Go with and stay with heartfelt feelings. They can, very often, tell you what's best for you. When you intercept feelings with a critical mind you can sabotage your own insights before they have a chance to surface.

2. *Let go of attachments to what is familiar.* By definition, new possibilities for change are not going to look "reasonable" immediately. And some of them are going to sound extremely strange to your inner critic. For example, if you repeatedly picture yourself leaving a "good" job or a "good" marriage, it's time to look into the situation. In the Third Space the feelings surrounding those thoughts can communicate their messages with full strength—and without constant interruption from a reasonable self.

3. *Observe what is there, not what you think should be there.* We all know that love is blind, but that doesn't mean that it doesn't see well. It means that it sees what is there exceptionally well because it's blind to what it's supposed to see. This insight (seeing within) blinds the lover and beloved to everything but their own heartfelt truth. Similarly, in the Third Space you can observe what is there and disregard what your rational mind tells you should be there.

4. *Relinquish control over who you are and the way things are supposed to be.* Clinging to outmoded patterns and beliefs as if they were parts of a wrecked lifeboat will only allow present dynamics to perpetuate themselves. You'll thrash about in the same waters holding onto the same old flotsam and jetsam, waiting to be saved.

   In the Third Space you will take the leap of faith that allows you to let go and let the waters wash you safely ashore. Sound farfetched? It isn't. Only when you take the risk of relinquishing control of who you are and the way things are supposed to be will you be able to recreate and reinvest yourself in a new cycle of growth. In the Third Space, this unlikely notion is the truth of the matter—it makes no difference how implausible the specifics are. Allowing yourself to be carried along by the attributes of the heart is a key point here.

5. *Give up the notion that the future has to be a repetition of the past.* The future you think up is only an *idea* about the future—it is not the true future. The past and the future are connected by the present moment, which is alive. In this alive moment, it is necessary to give up thinking about the future in terms of past values and desires. Possibilities for growth are limited when they are tied to preconceptions. In the Third Space, it is possible to imagine the future as infinitely clear and luminous without becoming attached to specific events and circumstances.

The Gifts of Perception

With these basic rules in mind, you will be able to focus your awareness on intuition, love, compassion, devotion, trust, and receptivity. Prepare yourself in your own time, with an affirmation that invites the Inner Guides to bring you the Gifts of Perception. These gifts are especially necessary in the Third Space, which is a place of origins and new beginnings, a place where a new cycle of growth can be spawned. The Gifts of Perception will strengthen a willingness to change so that it can become a powerful and effective force for positive growth later on.

Start by relaxing and centering yourself. Let go of fears and doubts and replace them with inner harmony. See and feel yourself surrounded by a circle of radiant energy. Silently (or aloud) repeat the affirmation.

Gifts of Perception

Eva, Kendra, Nixa, Belinda, Diana, and Erika,
be with me as I open my heart

to your wisdom and guidance.
Bring me the Gifts of Perception
so that my eyes open clearly,
my heart opens lovingly, my mouth opens
wisely, and my hands open powerfully.
Bring me:
Spontaneity,
Warmheartedness,
Tolerance,
Curiosity,
and a love of life.

Guide and protect me
as I am newborn in my powers.

6

~

Intuition

Intuition is a holistic intelligence that, once activated, will allow you to recognize a wide range of possibilities in situations and experiences.

The intuition not only *knows* for certain, it acts on that knowledge instead of disregarding it. This does not mean that you always act *only* on intuition, but rather that you can, if you want, pair it with what is already known.

What is intuition? How can I recognize, understand, and use it in my best interest? How can I *trust* my intuition? How can I deepen my intuitive powers? What are the "blocks" that can obstruct my intuitive awareness? How can I use intuition to make decisions? How can body awareness help me? How can I experience who I really am? How can I protect myself from someone else's anger? How can I use my intuitive powers to see the hidden patterns and possibilities in my life? What can I do when I want to reach out to others? How can I experience a future in which my core energy is more alive? These and other questions relating to intuition as a feminine way of empowerment will be answered in this chapter.

Intuition is an intelligence that comes to you through extraordinary channels. Instead of recognizing situations and events by using a rational process, intuition recognizes patterns and possibilities that are not readily apparent to the everyday thinking mind. By using intuition, it's possible to pick up vibes, get an inkling or a glimmer, a feeling in your bones, a premonition, a suspicion, a hunch—and from this sixth sense, you can arrive at a "second sight." This added insight, or a second way of looking at things, can be used to perceive, discern, comprehend, and grasp experiences, situations, and feelings. It can be used to solve problems, to illuminate the past, and to apprehend the future. Ultimately, you can use intuition alone or, as is more often the case, you can combine it with reason to arrive at conclusions, take risks, or perform tasks to achieve goals.

When you are attuned to your intuitive powers, you can discover what it is you need for your evolvement. Each person's life path is unique. You may find out that you need to enjoy your body more, or work on being generous, or make a commitment to a love relationship, or devote yourself more to serving others. One woman's path will take her to a place where she needs to form attachments. Another woman will be at a place where she needs to let go. You and you alone know what is right for you at this time. When you put aside rationalizations, justifications, and explanations, your intuition will lead you to a new awareness. From this place, right choices and decisions can be made.

Deepening Your Intuitive Powers

Let's begin in the Third Space with a series of exercises, and then move out of the Third Space into the everyday world where you can *use* your newfound abilities in practical ways.

In the Third Space, you will be concerned only with reaching within to remember and release your intuition. In this place, it is enough to open the heart, witness responses, and *feel* energy flowing in an affirmative direction. You will learn to fully awaken your intuitive powers in the Third Space exercises.

After completing each of the exercises, you will become more aware of your intuition and more able to understand its power. At that time you will learn how to move out of the Third Space and direct your energies into everyday situations, experiences, and relationships. In concrete terms, let's say your intuition has told you that your lover's passivity is the basic issue that's preventing you from getting closer. Intuitive awareness is just the first step, however. It is necessary to act on this intelligence by directing positive energy to the situation.

Setting your intuition in motion activates its power. And the more you use it, the stronger and more vital it becomes.

Third Space Exercises

Begin with a loving attitude toward yourself. Look at your successes and failures and see them with a compassionate understanding. View the present moment as a gift. Clear your mind of all thoughts and fears and begin to live fully in the present.

Realize that there may be many obstacles that prevent or limit you from deepening your intuition. But whenever you encounter negativity or come to an impasse, it can be offset by repeating the Gifts of Perception affirmation and by consulting with your inner Guide.

The Third Space Exercises are:

The Golden Ball—a visualization that will help you use intuition in making a decision.

Body Awareness—two exercises that you can use to tune into your intuitive perceptions about yourself and another person.

Mirror, Mirror—a visualization that presents you with a reflection of who you are and how you intuitively see yourself and your growth.

Imaging the Future—an exercise that will enable you to use your intuition to see a future in which you can reach out to others.

After completing each exercise, you will expand the experience by working through the sections that follow: Becoming Clearer and Empowerment. Both of these are simple ways for you to bring the observations from the exercises into your everyday world and use them in practical ways.

Making Decisions

Decision making covers a lot of bases. Getting your love relationship on more stable ground, leaving a dead-end job, having a baby, making new friends, or using leisure time more productively—all require making choices. In computerlike fashion, the mind some-times instantly pairs intuition with reason, and with lightning speed the decision is obvious and can be made easily. At other times, you can be perfectly reasonable about your choice—and yet feel that something's missing. The decision you arrive at doesn't feel right. Because you've left intuition out of the decision-making process. You are operating on the limited information that objectivity supplies.

But intuition is much more than a tool for problem solving. Its real power resides in giving you messages about your capabilities. And the messages tell you that using your intuitive powers leaves you more capable, more confident, and creates more possibilities for enriching your life.

Making decisions can *always* benefit from intuitive understanding. Even seemingly clear-cut and objective choices need to be tempered by what you already know on a deeper level. Something as simple as selling an out-of-town rental property because it isn't bringing in enough money can have other considerations and feelings attached to it when you *feel* the intuitive aspects. Perhaps you'll find out that you want to have emotional roots in the town, or that you can picture yourself retiring there, or that you would enjoy remodeling the house and re-leasing it at a higher rent.

When you start to feel the power of intuition and acknowledge and trust it as an intelligence you can use every day, any feelings of inadequacy or helplessness about making decisions will disappear. The more you use intuition, the more you empower it to create a strong basis for important choices in your life. The power of intuition is *your* power—but only if you let it work for you.

The Golden Ball

The first exercise is a visualization called *The Golden Ball.* You will enter the Third Space with Erika as your Guide. The visualization will help you to use intuition in making a decision.

The Golden Ball

Relax your body and close your eyes.
With Erika as your Guide, move deep
into the Third Space, a place where new
possibilities are born. Go deep, deep
within, as if going into a deep forest. Feel
your awareness expanding. With Erika as your
Guide, picture yourself coming into the center of
a clearing. Feel your awareness expanding.

If there is a decision to be made in your life,
let it surface here. Allow all the images and
thoughts and feelings surrounding the decision to
rise up as mist rises from the ground. Observe them. (Pause.)

Sense new possibilities and implications. (Pause.)
See clearly whatever has not been accessible to
you before. (Pause about two minutes.)

As your Guide, Erika intuitively gives you more
information about your decision. Listen to what
she says. (Pause.)

Before moving out of the Third Space, Erika gives
you a golden ball, which you hold in the palm of
your hand. Notice the ball. (Pause.)

Remember that you can return to this place
whenever you wish. Return now to your usual
waking reality, bringing with you everything you have
understood.

Intuition

Getting clearer

Whatever the decision is, it's important to you. Whether it's choosing to adopt a child, trying to make new friendships, taking early retirement, or getting sexually involved with a married man, you want to pick one course of action over another. Deep in your heart you know that logic and reason alone cannot bring the answer. To make the right choice, you also have to rely on your intuition.

In The Golden Ball visualization, what were your feelings as you moved deep within the Third Space? Serene? Apprehensive? Expectant? Numb? Frightened? Courageous?

As the images, thoughts, and feelings surfaced, were you able to observe them without interfering? Did you give yourself enough time to notice your feelings? Were you anxious? Worried? Calm? Angry? Sad?

What are the new possibilities and implications that you sensed? Is there anything that is holding you back from acting on this new understanding? Is there anything more you need to know in order to take the right action?

What were your feelings when Erika gave you the golden ball? Did you respond intuitively? Do you value Erika's gesture?

What was the most important thing you have understood about making your decision? To act with intuitive awareness, what emotional risks will it be necessary for you to take?

Empowerment

Empowering your intuition means that you give it a nod of approval. You're authorizing it to speak for you—and the more it does, the more valuable it becomes. Intuition is, by definition, a gut feeling that's panned out. There's a feeling of certainty involved, although you can't say for sure *why* you feel so sure about it. When you know something intuitively, you just do—and that's all there is to it.

Once you start to trust your intuition, you'll begin to delegate more and more authority to it. As you become more aware of how beneficial the messages are, your intuition will become more than a lucky hunch that pays off.

In the decision-making process, you can empower intuition by allowing it to have as much say as reason. Trust that it will guide you to the truth. Believe that there's a part of you that can go above and *beyond* what your rational mind observes.

With Erika as your Guide, empower intuition to help you in the decision-making process. Allow yourself to *experience* your intuition, not only in isolated moments but also as you go about making decisions in your daily routine. Intuition is sometimes a thunderbolt out of the blue. More often it is a skill that can be developed and *used* constantly to make choices in everyday life.

Body Awareness

Most of us are familiar with body language, certain body movements that "say" what is really on our mind. And we all know how to pick up vibes, especially when they are intensely positive or negative. Loving, peaceful vibes are easy to spot—a calm, centered person will exude tranquility. On the other hand, if a person is very angry and resentful, that message will be obvious from his or her demeanor without a word spoken. Negative vibes come out of the body like little daggers, and the eyes are filled with hostility.

It takes a little more skill and practice to "read" someone when they're astute at covering up the real message they want to give you. Reading between the lines can sometimes be exhausting, especially when someone is giving you conflicting messages that are completely at odds with each other. For example, your sister-in-law's conversation is friendly and pleasant, but her vibes, her angry, strident body movements and the way that she is stingy about putting food on the table, give you another message: she is hostile, envious, and emotionally withholding. When you look farther into how you are reading her, you begin to see that on a verbal level, you are contacting the cheerful person she wants to present to the world. On a nonverbal, intuitional level, you are contacting the person she wishes to dump on you—with all her jealousy, anger, and resentment pouring forth like a polluted river that's making its way into your backyard. Talking to these two separate selves is like talking to a person with two heads. You don't know which one to address. And the two separate selves very often haven't been introduced to each other. They can operate independently within the same person. And it's possible for the cheerful self to disown the angry self so it doesn't even recognize it's part of the same whole.

It's one thing to see something as it is—it's quite another to act on your intuition. Looking at what is going on in yourself and the other person is especially important in love relationships, work situations, and mother/child relationships. If these are the containers into which your major life effort is placed, it is necessary to examine what's been put into them.

When you become attuned to the tensions the body holds, the messages it gives out, and the rhythm of its movements, your intuition will guide you farther, and you can empower it by acting on what you now know. Empowerment does not always involve outer action or confrontation. You can choose a course of outward nonaction, while at the same time resolving the issue inwardly. Let's say that through body awareness, your intuition tells you that your new boss has a low opinion of women as managers. You've noticed his mannerisms are different when he talks to women than when he talks to men. His hand motions, the tilt of his head, and his general vibes tell you that he finds it degrading to deal with women in business situations. But, being the well-trained executive that he is, things on a verbal level are smooth.

You don't necessarily have to rush out and get another job (although that choice is always available). Empowerment in this case means that taking inner action on your part will allow you to remain in complete control of the situation, *despite* what is being conveyed to you by your boss. When you accept what is being dished out, you and your boss are in a nonverbal collusion that says, "Yes, women are unfit as managers." When you accept his communication, you make an agreement on this with him. Over a period of time, you can accept these communications over and over again—and each time you become more and more drained and helpless.

In this case, *do not accept* what your boss is offering. *Feel* that you don't accept it. Your own body responses will act naturally—it's not necessary to even think about them anymore. Your intuition has pointed out what is unacceptable and your body language will determine its own method of saying what's on your mind.

In the above example, the boss is a man. But it could very well be a woman. Remember that women can also carry erroneous beliefs and attitudes about themselves, and they too can communicate these destructive notions to you on a nonverbal level.

Being intuitively aware of your own body and its inner rhythms is a prerequisite to getting in touch with another person. The following exercises will enable you to fine-tune your perceptions. In Body Awareness I, you will use your intuition to get a better sense of who you are at this very moment. In Body Awareness II you will look at someone else with intuitive understanding to see beyond superficial assessments.

Remember when you are doing the exercises that you are in the Third Space. In this place, it is enough to open the heart, witness responses, and *feel* energy flowing. The Third Space is a place of new possibilities; it is not a place for interpretation. After completing each exercise, you will move on to Becoming Clearer and Empowerment. Taking these next steps will allow you to expand and elaborate on the experience you had in the Third Space.

Your Inner Guide will be a felt presence in many of the exercises. See, feel, understand, and welcome this presence as you would welcome your own insightful nature.

Body Awareness I

Stand comfortably with your feet shoulder-width apart.
Relax your body. With Erika as your Guide,
witness your breath.
Observe your heartbeat.
Feel your life pulse.
Notice where your body feels strain.
Feel where your body is most alive.

Direct your attention to the whole body.
witness the energy that is being released.

Intuition

If there are colors, observe them.
Feel your pulsating life energy as it
travels into the surrounding atmosphere.

At this time, begin to intuitively understand
the message your body is sending. (Pause about
two minutes.) You can return to this place anytime.

Listen now to what Erika intuitively understands about
your body and your life energy. (Pause.)

Return to your usual alertness, bringing with you a
newfound awareness of your body.

Getting clearer

In witnessing your breath, was it deep and relaxed? Shallow?
Regular? Silent? Noisy? Free flowing? Controlled? Could you feel
your heartbeat? Was it strong? Loud? Soft? Was your life pulse
quick? Slow? Alive? Sluggish? Where did your body feel strain?
Did it feel tense? Overburdened? Painful? Disabled? Tight? Where
did your body feel most alive? Did it feel energized? Capable?
Courageous? Inspired? Joyful?

When you directed your attention to your whole body, was the
released energy powerful? Exciting? Active? Optimistic? Caring?
Confident? Drifting? Aggressive? Creative? Depressed? Scattered?

When you felt your life energy travel into the surrounding
atmosphere, did it grow more powerful? Become inert? Diffuse?
Change from active to passive? Did your life energy make the
atmosphere around you more highly charged?

Was there a color connected with the energy? Did you sense that
the color was cheerful? Melancholy? Healing? Angry? Spiritual?
Jealous? Compassionate? Afraid? Courageous? Imaginative? Pes-
simistic?

What was the most important thing that you intuitively understood about the message your body was sending? What was the

most important thing that Erika told you about your body and your life energy? What more do you sense you need to know about your body to release strain and feel more alive?

Empowerment

Awareness of your body is essential to understanding yourself. It is important to be able to read your own body messages correctly. Very often we think our bodies are saying one thing, when, in fact, they can be saying the opposite.

At first, it may be necessary to make a deliberate effort to become more attuned to what your body is telling you. You may be taking in a lot of negativity from other people or unsuccessfully extending your loving concern to heal the wounds of others, or you may be sending out your own vital and energetic life force into the surrounding atmosphere so that all those around you are recharged.

Body awareness is the first step in transmitting the *rhythm* of who you are—quiet and tranquil, fast and nervous, and so forth. Your life rhythm can be healing or creative. It can bounce, soar, and zing. It can bubble like a mountain spring or it can be as flat as stale ginger ale. The body's rhythm doesn't lie, but it is up to you to understand its truth.

To empower your intuitive perceptions about your body, get to know them first and then apply them. Let's say you've found out that your body feels strain in the shoulders, and you liken it to trying to protect yourself from harm. Your body communicates that to those around you. In your love relationship, you realize that your attitude toward your lover is one in which you feel you have to protect yourself from possible harm. Through contemplation, consulting with your guide, and talking with your lover about the issue, you come to understand that your protective stance comes from a generalized fear of possible harm rather than from anything concrete. You notice that the strain in your shoulders lessens as the unnecessary protection of yourself is allowed to drop.

As your body awareness and intuition become more developed, you will be able to reach out with what you know and touch all your relationships—and the wider world around you.

In the following exercise, you will use your intuitive powers to understand another person's aliveness. Remain observant rather than judgmental. Expect that your intuition will provide you with the impressions you need. (To get the most benefit from the exercise, try it first with someone you don't know very well.)

Body Awareness II

Sit directly opposite your partner. Breathe slowly,
deeply. With Erika as your Guide, center yourself
by focusing your attention on the solar plexus,
about an inch or two above the navel. As you inhale,
draw energy into the area. As you exhale, let
the energy flow out into the surrounding atmosphere.

Look at your partner. Observe the eyes. Hands.
Feet. Legs. Groin. Chest. Neck.
Shoulders. Mouth. Ears. Hair.
Notice the whole body.

Become aware of your partner's energy.
Sense energy patterns and colors without
interpreting them.
Observe the energy flow.

Notice areas in your own body where
you feel refreshed. Notice areas where
you feel drained.
Observe where peacefulness occurs in your body.
Observe agitation. (Pause about two minutes.)

Sense the message your partner's body is giving.

Listen to what Erika intuitively tells you about
your partner's life force.
Before returning to your usual awareness,
stabilize and protect yourself by allowing
your body to accept only what you agree to.

Getting clearer

When you looked at your partner, what did you observe about the different parts of his or her body? What did you notice about the whole body?

How would you describe your partner's energy? Was it intense? Calm? Warm? Cool? Active? Passive?

How would you describe the energy flow? Weak? Fast? Slow?

Where in your own body did you feel refreshed? Where did you feel drained? Peaceful? Agitated?

What message did you sense that your partner's body was giving? How did your body respond?

What did Erika tell you about your partner's life force?

What was the most useful thing you brought back from the exercise? How will it be useful? How can you use this to reach out to others? How can you use it to protect yourself?

Empowerment

You can use your intuition about another person's basic nature to reach out to him or her with encouragement, love, concern, tenderness, and care. When you see the basic nature that extends beyond personality and culturally learned attitudes, you can create an interchange that is deeply vital.

On an ordinary day, you can sense, look, and listen to what lies outside your usual conditioned and judgmental way of seeing others. The essential self is far more alive and important than the socially approved presentation of ourselves. It takes courage to acknowledge your own basic nature and to respond to another person's essence, rather than his or her acquired nature. But it is a skill that you can develop easily. Take the time in ordinary experiences with a friend, lover, or child to focus on and become intuitively aware of what your bodies are saying—and become attuned also to what your body is accepting.

Intuitive perceptions about another person also allow you to protect yourself against everything you don't agree to accept. On an energy level, people are constantly sending out vibes of all kinds, and your body can take in and absorb depression, anger, agitation, discontent, fear, etc. Very often that's why you feel tired after spending time with a person whose inner state is distressed. Similarly, you can feel uplifted, inspired, and energized when your companion sends out warm, generous, and loving body messages. Peaceful energy and strength can radiate through the fingertips in a handshake, and when you are introduced to someone whose basic nature is alive and vital, that person's energy is apparent immediately.

The idea is to create balance and harmony within yourself so that you are aware of your own body, the other person's body, and you can sense the interchange of energy between you. Being alert to discordant messages from your friends doesn't mean that you discount what is going on. It means that your body observes and then protects itself.

You can protect yourself from the rage and discontent of others, and *at the same time,* if you want, reach out and give them your love. You can protect yourself by simply being aware and by allowing your body only to accept what it agrees to accept.

Remember, the vibes that other people give off belong to them. Stay in touch with your own positive life force when someone else wants to pass along their negativity. If your companion is someone that you want to help, your own affirmative stance and loving concern can counteract and dissolve even the most negative life energy. The Quaker saying, "All the darkness in the world cannot put out the light of one small candle," holds especially true here.

If you need help from another person, seek out someone who radiates healthy and wholesome energy. Go to a friend or family member you intuitively sense can give you the vitality you need.

Mirror, Mirror

In "Snow White" the question, "Mirror, mirror on the wall, tell me who is fairest of them all?" has more to do with inner beauty than outward appearances. In contrast to the Evil Queen, Snow White deals with life fairly—that is, authentically, honestly, justly, and candidly. She is impeccably fair-minded and shows herself to be courteous, gracious, agreeable, and polite. She is the "fairest in all the land," and like new snow, she is unblemished and pure. So far, so good. But, as we all know, there must be more to life. In the rest of the story, she turns out to have both pluck and luck. An updated version of the story could have her looking into the mirror after all her experiences with evil and asking, "Mirror, mirror do not hide, my other darker side." If Snow White could have seen both sides of her nature in the mirror, she could have seen who she really was at that very moment and made a more conscious choice about riding off with the Prince and living happily ever after in fairy tale land.

As the current slang goes (when the person addressed goes charmingly against expectations), "You're so bad!" There *is* some good in being bad.

So you're not a goody two-shoes (and you don't want to be). And you're not a dragon lady either. Then who are you—aside from the result of your own and other people's built-in perceptions? Snow White could go for a lifetime asking the mirror who is fairest, with the mirror always answering her name. Boring, eh? The trick is to ask other questions too.

Again remember that in the following exercise, Mirror, Mirror, you are in the Third Space. It is not necessary to make a judgment about who you are. Simply observe your reflection as you would observe the reflection of trees in a pond. All you need to do is notice all you can and feel the beating of your heart.

In this visualization, you will get an intuitive understanding of who you are. Your #1 Guide is the felt presence here.

Mirror, Mirror

Close your eyes and relax your body. Picture
yourself in a room. Notice your surroundings.
On the wall there is a full-length mirror.
It is an extraordinary mirror because it can reflect everything
exactly as it exists.

Walk directly in front of the mirror and
take time to observe your reflection.

Intuition

Ask the mirror to present you with an image
of yourself as a tree or plant or flower.
Observe the image carefully. Notice all
the details you can about the tree or
plant or flower. (Pause.)

Go deep within and sense its strengths. Get
to know its weaknesses. Picture its growth.
Stay with your impressions and reach within
for others. (Pause.)

Listen to what your #1 Guide intuitively understands
about the tree or plant or flower. (Pause.)

Return to your usual alertness, open your eyes
and stretch your body.

Alternate visualization

You can also do this visualization by asking the mirror to present
you with an image of yourself as an animal.

Getting clearer

Gaining intuitive understanding of who you are is a lifelong
endeavor. You can be aware of many different identity states, and
you can often go from one facet of yourself to another. But the
essence of who you are sometimes remains hidden. During this
visualization, you were able to see that you are far more than your
personality.

In the Mirror, Mirror visualization, what was the room like?
Was the mirror old or new? Was it plain or ornamented?

When you observed yourself in the mirror, what did you see?
Were you happy? Sad? Detached? Noncommittal?

When you asked the mirror to present you as a tree or plant or
flower (or animal), what did the mirror show you? Was the image
full and leafy? Sparse? Could you see flowers or fruit? Seeds?
(Furry? Powerful? Small and meek?)

What did you sense about the image? Was it growing straight and tall? Was it branching out?

What did your #1 Guide sense about the tree or plant or flower (or animal)?

What was the most important thing you brought back with you? What can help you right now with your relationship to yourself? With your relationship to others?

Empowerment

Empowering who you are involves *using* the impressions and images you received in Mirror, Mirror. During the visualization and afterward in Getting Clearer, an unfolding has taken place. You have peeled back the layers to see what exists. All your strengths and weaknesses can now be brought into balance and harmony in everyday life.

Whether you've been cranky and irritable with coworkers, disloyal to your friends, unable to concentrate, overtired, frustrated because your goals seem farther away than ever, or unhappy and overburdened with endless chores—you can still remain attuned to your basic nature.

While you are in the experience of, let's say, having a heart-to-heart talk with your lover or dealing with an envious friend, center yourself in the image presented to you by the mirror. *Use* all the beauty, strength, magnetism, colors, and rootedness of the tree or plant or flower (or animal). It reaches to the sun and to positive energy to grow, not to dark shadows. In a similar manner, you can reach out for what is affirming.

If your image appears unhealthy or stunted, begin to prune away the dead parts and help it grow. You can actually take a few seconds while you are in your ordinary experience to do this. In a few blinks of an eye, you can *feel* yourself strengthening the tree or plant or flower that is the essence of who you are.

Imaging the Future

It is important to think of the future not as a time when happiness will be achieved, but rather as a place where your basic nature can become more alive. When an oracle, astrologer, or psychic reveals the future, he or she predicts events according to what the stars (or other prophetic inspirations) foretell about events and circumstances. You also can use your intuitive powers to apprehend and comprehend what the future holds. Instead of trying to question what things will be like (Will I marry? Is travel in the cards? Can I expect riches? Will I be lucky in love?), it is more beneficial to gain intuitive knowledge into *who* you will be.

Through the popularity of books by Shirley MacLaine, Lynn Andrews, and others, the idea of past-life regressions and reincarnation experiences from other planes of existence are in the mainstream of popular thought today. Contacting the *future* by using your intuitive powers is just as powerful—and as possible.

By contacting another level of reality, you can observe yourself as you really are—not the socially approved presentation of yourself, but rather, your *essence*, the basic nature which is uniquely you. Remembering your past often involves gathering the different parts of yourself into a unified whole. Focusing on your future self (as we are concerned with it here) means that you will see your basic nature in another life space and *experience* it awakening and responding to its own aliveness. In this way, you will strengthen your core energy *in* the future and *for* the future. The idea is not to control or influence future events, it is to *preexperience* your basic nature and its positive energy.

Before you begin the visualization, Imaging the Future, let go of all beliefs about what is important and not important. Let go of your ideas about how things ought to be. Realize that material possessions and status do not always satisfy the need for something more vital.

This visualization is especially powerful because it combines the new possibilities of the Third Space with the newness of a future that can be more alive for you. Imaging the Future often brings extraordinary perceptions and results.

Here you will use intention to see yourself in a future that is alive and vibrant. Since Erika is the wise woman who can foresee and foretell, she is your Guide in the visualization. In Imaging the Future, she is a felt presence accompanying you on a journey into the future.

Imaging the Future

Close your eyes, begin to unwind your body.
With Erika as your Guide, draw attention to
your breath. On the exhalation, let go of
everyday concerns. On the inhalation, bring
fresh, clean, clear energy into every part
of your body! (Continue two more times.)

On the exhalation, let go of the past.
On the inhalation, bring in revitalizing energy.
(Continue one more time.)

Breathe deeply. On the outgoing breath,
allow yourself to let go of the present.
On the incoming breath, allow yourself
to take in new and crystal clear energy.
(Continue one more time.)

You are ready to travel now to the future.
Your breath will carry you there.
The future is another life space. It is a place
where you can feel yourself awaken to
dormant positive energy. In this life space
you can preexperience the aliveness that
will be yours.

Take in a deep breath. On a deep, slow exhalation,
make the journey and arrive at your future.
Take time to notice your surroundings. As you
inhale, replenish yourself with cool, clear air.
Feel yourself alert and alive with energy.
As you exhale, feel your life breath extending
far, far into the future. Begin to experience
your life energy as timeless. Intuitively, feel
yourself connected to the eternal forces of the
universe. (Pause about two minutes.)

Return now refreshed and energized to your usual
awareness.

Getting clearer

In one word, how would you describe the surroundings in your future space? Cramped? Spacious? Dark? Sunny? Luxurious? Sparse? Were the colors bright? Muted?

When you extended your life breath far into the future, could you *feel* yourself expanding into an unknown area?

When you experienced your life energy as timeless, did you *feel* yourself going beyond personal realms?

When you felt yourself connected to the eternal forces of the universe, did you *feel* yourself linked to infinite possibilities? Was it possible for you to take a step beyond, to the brink of new horizons?

Empowerment

Use the *feelings* of limitless potential to empower your future. All of the future and all of the past is present in this very moment, and *only* this instant is alive with possibilities for becoming all that you can be. The future unfolds on its own, but it is you that brings to it beliefs, attitudes, and ways of being. Some of them will help you transcend limitations; others will stand in the way of your evolvement.

The idea here is not to control the future, but to make yourself more alive *in* it by opening *to* it in this very moment. In daily life, this can be done by creating an attitude of expectant awareness. With a *feeling* of optimistic anticipation, you can deal creatively with love problems, work-related stress, feelings of inadequacy, depression, and disappointments. Expanding your awareness into the *potential* of your future means that you choose to see its limitless possibilities right at this very moment.

In this chapter, many of the exercises are visualizations. Intuition and visualizations go hand in hand, since intuition is best realized by the use of images to unlock its potential. The ability to create images as a mental representation of reality is one of the mind's most profound talents. Each of the visualizations is very different; however, they all allow you leeways and give you insights that are not possible in ordinary consciousness. Certain kinds of knowledge simply cannot be understood when wishes and desires are in command, or when you are reacting to your culturally approved (but sometimes inauthentic) self. As Shakespeare said, "This above all: to thine own self be true." But it's easy to put up barriers to the essential self. Disappointments and threats to inner stability (and many other life shocks) can cause your basic nature to remain hidden and inactive.

The exercises are a way of transcending your own and cultural limitations. They clear distortions and free energy so that you can become far more than you are now. Becoming more aware of your intuitive powers, becoming clearer about your perceptions, and empowering intuition so that you remain wide awake and alert in both your inner and outer worlds—all mean that you will begin to see your life from a different perspective.

Finding out who you are and how you can reach out to others by using your intuitive powers often means giving up cherished beliefs about yourself and outmoded images about what the future holds. When you change, the world around you changes, and you can begin to accept life as it unfolds—and allow your intuition to guide your heart. In all of this, your inner Guide is a felt presence that you can call on when you need to.

Continue, in your own time, to the next chapter—Compassion, Love, and Devotion. Again, the Third Space exercises are just the right combination that will enable you to transcend your limitations and make the most of your innate capacity to love.

7

Compassion, Love, and Devotion

Compassion, love, and devotion, over the centuries, have always been thought of as "womanly." But what does devotion mean in today's world? Is love merely a leftover word from some romantic, medieval ideal of courtly love? One that involves a princess with a problem and a rescuing knight? Is compassion out of date, or is it natural to empathize with others?

True compassion, love, and devotion involve intimacy. Their age-old forms and expressions have undergone radical changes in the last decade. The images we have held as absolutes no longer work as they did previously. Real intimacy between people (partners, friends, family members, etc.) now means it is necessary to form a new model of reality, or better yet, a *pattern* of change in which compassion, love, and devotion play a major part in everyday life.

New ways of understanding compassion, love, and devotion are needed in today's world. They've outgrown their old forms and must be retrieved and revived as a pattern in daily life that creates authentic intimacy between people.

To bring out the best in each other, love is what works. Compassion is what works. Devotion works. They are all alive within you—creatively vital and able to honor the kind of life you want to lead with your partner, friends, and family. When love works, it feels alive. And when compassion and devotion are alive, new possibilities of mutual appreciation present themselves.

Begin, in your own time, by acknowledging your inner resources for compassion. Understand that a loving self resides in you at this very moment. Realize that devotion to your Inner Feminine means that you respect your Inner Feminine Powers, and that you are loyal and steadfast in *not denying* that these powers can be activated at your discretion.

In this chapter, you will learn to use Active Contemplation. This is a way of mindfully observing and remembering your genuine feminine self. As you become more aware of your true feelings and your reactions to the world, any obstacles to developing your full powers of compassion, love, and devotion will dissolve.

In each of the Active Contemplation exercises, you will start with yourself. You will develop compassion for yourself, love for yourself, and you will become more devoted to the *value* of your Inner Feminine Power. Paying attention to yourself is the beginning of self-understanding. From there, compassion, love, and devotion toward others can naturally evolve.

It may seem like the easiest thing in the world to be kind to yourself, to love yourself, and be devoted to discovering your inner powers. But resistance sneaks in. It is quite amazing how hard it is to spend time deliberately liking yourself. Your essential feminine self is marvelously beautiful. It has to be nourished and cared for and allowed to grow splendidly. But paying attention to that often-neglected part of yourself can create enormous resistance.

Active Contemplation will allow you to contact resistance to nourishing your Inner Feminine—and it will allow you to observe it, understand it, and overcome it. To have compassion toward yourself is vital. To love yourself is vital. To be devoted to discovering how and when and where your Inner Feminine Power can be activated is vital.

The next step, after paying attention to yourself, is to extend yourself to others. Extend your compassion, your love, your devotion. Pour out all that you are. When you develop the capacity to be attentive to yourself, it is a fairly easy transition to learning to be attentive to others in the deepest possible way. With the help of Active Contemplation and your Guide, the way will be clear.

In this chapter, there are six Active Contemplation exercises. They are to be done once a week or so. But you can return to them at any time. The exercises are:

Compassion
- Remembering Compassion
- Boundless Light of Understanding

Love
- Morning Liking and Loving
- Expressing Love

Devotion
- Guiding Thread
- Channeling Devotion

All the Active Contemplation exercises will be done in the Third Space, a place of rebirth. In the Third Space, new channels to your Inner Feminine are created, new motivations and hopes, new boundaries and limits, and new self-images are born. Take a moment now to close your eyes and feel that you are in this place of renewal.

Trust in your capacity to grow.

Compassion

To most people, compassion means a sympathetic understanding of the suffering of others and a desire to help them. When you drop coins into a homeless beggar's cup, you might feel some fleeting compassion that disappears almost immediately as you take the next few steps away. When a photograph of an AIDS victim in a magazine captures your attention for a moment, compassionate feelings may surface. In daily life, there can be many impersonal confrontations in which compassionate feelings arise. But compassion for those who are closest to you may be limited or lacking altogether.

In this section, you will learn how compassion can be cultivated in a way that opens you to your own natural loving self. This loving self is empathic, and it emotionally recognizes another person's depression, loneliness, fears, etc. The loving self wants to help a friend, a partner, a child, or a coworker alleviate emotional or physical suffering. By practicing Active Contemplation, you'll find a loving self that feels safe and comfortable with its natural desire to help others.

In your own time, begin the Active Contemplation exercises. To practice the exercises, simply read them and allow yourself to open to their meaning. With mindfulness and watchfulness, stay awake (that's the "active" part) and observe and reflect on (that's the "contemplation" part) whatever surfaces from within. If you like, your Guide (whichever one you choose) can be with you as a felt presence in each of the exercises.

In the following exercise, you will begin to evoke feelings of compassion by building on a previous experience of kindness and closeness. Remembering a time when someone was kind to you is the first step in actively developing compassion. Self-observation and self-remembering allow you to contact the often neglected aspects of your compassionate nature—and your feminine authority.

Remembering Compassion

For now, close yourself to all that is troubling you.

Find a quiet place in your heart that is filled with good memories.

Remember a time of struggle when someone helped you in a compassionate way.

Return to that time and reexperience the feeling of being cared for with intelligent, effective compassion.

Notice any resistance to being loved. Observe it as
you would observe a cloud, and then allow it to
dissolve. For now, rid yourself of all obstacles to
being loved. Allow obstacles, one by one, to melt
away.

Focus on being loved by another person. Take time to
feel the kindness and compassion that you received.
(Pause.)

Realize how worthwhile you are to be loved in this
way. Stay with the good feelings you have about
yourself, rather than fears and doubts.

Take time to feel the effects of compassionate
gestures, words, and acts.

Return to your everyday awareness knowing that
it is possible to extend compassion to all beings:
people who treat you well, people who treat you
neutrally, and those who treat you badly.

In the exercise below, you will extend your compassion to another
person. You will experience the compassion that already exists
within you as boundless light radiating from your heart, and you
will experience compassion for others as boundless light radiating
from your mind.

Boundless Light of Understanding

Clear your heart, mind, and body of all that stands
in the way of practicing compassion.

Feel that your love and generosity will be accepted by
others, not rejected.

Realize that it is all right to try to alleviate another
person's suffering, even if what you try doesn't work.

Begin now to experience the feeling of compassion. In
your mind's eye, see a friend who would benefit from your

compassion. Send your love and compassion to this person.
Feel compassion radiate from your heart in boundless light.
Feel compassion radiate from your mind in boundless light.
Feel that you are both bathed in the strong, warm light
of your compassion.

If you encounter any resistance, remember
to observe it, and then allow it to dissolve.

Begin to observe your feelings.
Feel the effects of your true compassionate nature. (Pause.)

Realize that the compassionate heart and the
compassionate mind are one reality. In this reality,
one's joy for others is supreme.

Return now to everyday consciousness, bringing with you
everything you need to compassionately help others.

Love

Love can be defined in hundreds of ways, many of them poetic. In
this chapter, we'll say that love is strong affection for another
person—a husband or lover, a friend, child, etc. When love is
actualized by two people, it is expressed through words and
gestures. The experience of love creates an intimate bond that is
subtle and immensely significant.

The ways in which a man and woman approach each other in a
love relationship have changed dramatically over the last several
decades—but the meaning of love remains the same. In general,
women no longer start a relationship or get married with only the
idea that they're going to live happily ever after. And men are no
longer inclined to take on the role of sole breadwinner. But a
coupled life still means that security and contentment are important,
and that the things that are alive and creatively generative between
two people are what hold the relationship together.

Parent/child relationships are becoming stronger as more and
more women are putting their careers on hold while they take time

Compassion, Love, and Devotion

out to give their children traditional mother love. Many women are beginning to understand that nothing they were doing professionally was as important as raising their young children.

In a friendship, love means sharing your courage and your frailties with someone you really care about.

At your own pace, begin the Active Contemplation exercises, which will help put you in touch with loving feelings. In these exercises you will remember how it feels to love and *like* yourself, and then you will extend your love to those around you.

Any resistance you encounter can be deactivated in the exercise.

The next exercise takes only three minutes each morning, but the effects are cumulative. In this Active Contemplation exercise you will start each day on a positive note by beginning to like yourself. You can practice this exercise by lying in bed just after you wake up, or standing in front of the bathroom mirror, or while you are enjoying your coffee. In the morning your mind is less cluttered than it is as the day goes on. When you are refreshed from a night's sleep, the exercise can have a very beneficial, almost self-hypnotic effect.

This is a very simple but powerful practice, and it's designed to put you on good terms with yourself as you start the day.

Morning Liking and Loving

Begin by smiling at who you are. Smile
at how you came to this place on your life path.

Take a moment to focus on your breathing. Breathe
deeply and naturally. On the inhalation, breathe in
happiness. On the exhalation, breathe out discontentment
and anxiety. (Continue for one minute.)

Now begin to genuinely like yourself. (Pause.) As you
like yourself more and more, now begin to love yourself.
(Pause.) Believe that you are a person who deserves to be
loved—and love who you are at this very moment.

If you encounter resistance, observe it
as you would observe the ocean, then allow the resistance
to dissolve and fade away.

With conviction in your voice, say aloud, "I really like myself."

When you creatively experience liking yourself in the Morning Liking and Loving exercise, you begin the day by giving love to yourself. Throughout the day, try to stay with the feelings of liking yourself. In any one day, it is easy to become frustrated, disappointed, or angry at yourself for a lot of reasons. And it's easy to protect yourself from suffering by denying what you feel—about yourself and others. Sometimes, instead of opening up and giving love, it's possible to react mechanically by closing down and not allowing yourself to be vulnerable. Your defenses take over, despite your best intentions.

Instead of *re*acting, it's possible to *act* from feelings of love. Learning to *be mindful* of liking yourself in everyday life, and learning to *trust* the accompanying feelings, will provide you with a basis so that eventually you can extend your love to everyone.

After you have practiced the Morning Liking and Loving exercise for a few days, you can practice the next exercise, Expressing Love at any time. This Active Contemplation exercise was designed to help you expand your capacity to love. Gradually, you will be able to extend your love unconditionally to those around you. And remember, when you can fully experience and express love, you will attract people with the same traits.

Resistance (and other barriers and obstacles) to expressing love can be counteracted by observing them and then dissolving whatever is limiting or preventing you from actualizing love (the most complex, yet simple, of all the Inner Feminine Powers).

Expressing Love can significantly change your life in a positive way. Look at all the aspects of yourself in day-to-day situations and be mindful and watchful. Notice changes when they occur. These may be changes in self-perception, in attitude, or in the ways that you deal with people, relationships, or situations.

We all have many facets to ourselves and our identities. When love goes out to whatever is wonderful and beautiful, as well as to what isn't so wonderful and beautiful, then love is all-encompassing. Nothing is denied. Nothing is split off, buried, or repressed, no matter how unpleasant, fearful, or shameful.

Compassion, Love, and Devotion

In your own time, begin the Expressing Love exercise. You can return to it as a routine practice, or whenever anger, jealousy, resentment, or fear have replaced the love that is in your heart. The exercise will help reconnect you with love and its transformative power.

Expressing Love

Begin by centering yourself in the love you have
for yourself. Feel it as a warm light radiating from
within. Feel its warmth and light surround you. (Pause.)
Experience the feeling of love. (Pause.)

Now, begin to extend your love to someone you know
—a friend, husband, child, lover, parent, coworker,
or a new acquaintance. In your mind's eye, picture that
person.

Expand your capacity to love by sending love to
another in a steady stream of white light.
Feel the light radiating from within. Feel its warmth
and light completely surround both of you.

Now, in any way you want, experience the feeling
of expressing your love. (Pause.) Experience the feeling
of expanding your capacity to love. (Pause.)

Stay with the feeling and extend your love to people
who have helped you. (Pause.) Now extend love to those
who have hurt you. (Pause.) Go even farther—expand your
capacity to love by extending your love to all beings.
(Pause.)

Believe that your love is limitless. Realize that your love
has the power to transform whatever it touches.

Devotion

When you are devoted, it means that you are loyal, faithful, and steadfast. Devotion requires ardor, enthusiasm, diligence, and perseverance. But devotedness in the outer world doesn't always correspond with devotion to your own inner resources. It's possible to devote yourself to a good cause (such as a political campaign, a school fund-raising effort, or a weight-loss diet), and at the same time deny the value of your Inner Feminine and its active, transformative power.

In this section you will look at devotion from within, not at the outer forms it presently takes. The first Active Contemplation exercise in this section, The Guiding Thread, will give you the opportunity to become more attached to your feminine powers and to respect and admire yourself for everything you are at this very moment. You will devote yourself to *your own* convictions of truth, beauty, and self-worth. Remember, at this point you are not looking at yourself from the outside. What you will get from The Guiding Thread exercise is an *inner* ability to claim your own feminine authority and devote yourself to it. Even though you may be actively presenting yourself to the world as a woman who is actualizing her feminine powers, *internally* these powers may not be fully valued and appreciated. To live fully, it is necessary to affirm a strong connection to your Inner Feminine and to feel a strong devotedness to all that you are.

From there, in your own time, continue with the second Active Contemplation exercise in this section, Channeling Devotion. Here you will take the next step and extend your devotion to others. This is a profound undertaking. It is filled with almost unlimited possibilities for enlightenment. Before you begin, a word of caution is necessary. Devotion is a *mindful* passion. Stay awake to exactly what and who you are devoting yourself to.

Remember that devotion is not an addiction to another person's attributes. Nor is it a dependent state.

Devotion is one of life's most rewarding qualities. Fidelity is a thin wire, but it is made of gold. In these exercises you will come in contact with the truth of your own steadfast nature, and you will learn to use the power it provides.

This exercise, The Guiding Thread, will lead you from a previous time of devotion to a present problem. Staying close to feelings of devotion to your own truth can help you respond with greater clarity and strength to almost any situation.

Compassion, Love, and Devotion

The Guiding Thread

Begin by remembering a time when you were loyal and true to your inner feminine self, despite what was happening around you. Reexperience the *feeling* of devotion to your own truth. (Pause.)

Stay with the feeling and mindfully observe how you respected or admired yourself at the time.

In your mind's eye, take a thread called The Guiding Thread and let it lead you to a present problem.

Staying with the feeling of devotion to your own truth, contemplate all aspects of the present situation, both positive and negative. (Pause.)

Stay with the feeling of devotion and accept whatever action (or nonaction) is necessary at this time.

Understand that devotion to your own truth will help you respond to almost any problem with greater clarity and strength.

Channeling Devotion

Begin with the image of a close friend (or lover). Extend your fond attachment and loyalty to her (or him). Go a step farther and feel your devotion increase.

Picture someone else, another person who has recently helped you with a problem or relationship. Expand your devotedness by extending your fond attachment and loyalty to that person. (Pause.)

If resistance occurs, remember to observe it, and then dissolve it.

Now, think about a work project you want to concentrate on. Channel loving commitment to the project by

focusing first on the project and then on your
devotion. In your mind's eye, see them as two separate
circles. Now, bring them slowly together until they
are one. (Pause.)

Lastly, reflect on a new life goal (such as
motherhood, overcoming addiction, or new love
relationship). Channel loving commitment to the
life goal by focusing first on the goal
and then on your devotion. In your mind's eye, see them as
two separate circles. Now, bring them slowly together
until they are one. (Pause.)

Realize that devotion can be channeled into other aspects
of your life in the same way. Understand that devotion
is an Inner Feminine Power that can enhance relationships
and promote communion and connectedness between people.

8

Trust

In this chapter, you will learn to trust your trust (an Inner Feminine Power that can open many doors in your life). As you become more trusting of yourself (and others), resentments fade, old wounds dissolve, and you can open yourself to the present moment and all that it has to offer.

Past experiences that are hurtful usually make people wary. And the more sensitive you are, the more hurt you can be. When you act in an open and generous way, you are giving from a deep Inner Feminine. It is a tender and vital part of your being, and when your love and care is rejected, you feel rejected on a very deep level.

As the years go by, it is possible to build up quite a repertoire of safe behavior patterns and feelings, so that eventually you can wall yourself off from your essential feminine nature. Staying defended means that your perceptions, thoughts, and feelings are ones that are "allowed" because they protect you from pain, frustration, and confusion. But, in the long run, this protection is an illusion. Your original and natural feminine self is a self where love and trust are present. Separating yourself from your true nature prevents you from channeling love and trust.

Venus Unbound

In the chapter on intuition, you learned to contact and use your intuition, and in Compassion, Love, and Devotion, you learned how to activate other feminine powers through Active Contemplation Exercises. In this chapter, you will take everything you've learned one step farther by using some of the exercises in actual day-to-day experiences.

Trust means that confidence, optimism, hope, reliability, and anticipation are all at work. In real terms, trust means that you can completely show your true nature (with all its shadows and warts) to another person and feel assured that nothing will ever be used against you. As you can see, it means that you show yourself as a vulnerable human being, one who lets true feminine essence replace automatic behavior, learned feelings, and mechanical habits. To trust is to live and live openly.

Living close to your inner feminine trust does *not* mean you will never be betrayed by a lover, a friend, a coworker. It does not mean that you won't experience pain, nor does it mean that your life will go more smoothly. But it *does* mean that you will be more alive and more energetic. Remember, it takes a lot of energy to constantly close yourself off from the deep inner feminine self that generates love and trust. It's a mistake to think that just because you don't consciously feel the drain of automated responses, they aren't there dulling your whole life.

When you begin to trust your heart, mind, and body, you begin to trust what makes you truly alive. In your heart, you can trust the love and hope that you feel for the future. In your mind, you can trust your decisions, plans, and goals. In your body, trust your sexual responses, cycles, and physical attunement to others.

What does this mean? It means you begin to rely on your Inner Feminine, your true nature, to *inform* you of *feelings*, and you can go with and stay with those feelings instead of dismissing them and attaching yourself to preprogrammed reactions.

There are four powerful exercises in this chapter. Again, remember when you practice them that you are in the Third Space, a place of renewal. When you do certain of these exercises in the presence of others, you may not be consciously aware of being in the Third Space. Nevertheless, whenever you prepare for important new connections to be made, you are in the Third Space (whether you are alone or with others).

Your Guide in each exercise is one of your choosing. Evoke her presence at the beginning of the exercise by simply calling upon her to be with you. Your Guide will be with you, and if necessary, you can call upon her for direction after you complete the exercise.

In the first exercise, Trust Your Trust, you will strengthen your authentic Inner Feminine by trusting in its power.

The next three exercises represent the Golden Triangle—the heart, mind, and body. And in each of these exercises, you will trust all that originates from your true and unique essence. It's basically a letting-go process. All that is stale and dry is cast away, and all that is authentic is trusted and relied upon.

As an example, let's say that in your love relationship you were afraid of intense feelings and successfully kept them hidden. You didn't trust your heart. Somehow you didn't let your heart *inform* you of your passion.

And let's say that you didn't trust the decisions and plans your mind offered. You dismissed the idea of taking the next step and getting closer to your lover. And you denied the messages your body was sending. You dismissed your sexual needs (or you dismissed exploring new and innovative sexual practices). Instead of trusting your body's responses, you ignored what it was telling you.

This is just one example of how mistrust of heart, body, and mind can stifle a relationship and prevent it from growing. In the exercises that follow, you will find whatever it is you need to trust yourself more fully, and you will activate the Inner Feminine Power of trust by actually practicing some of the exercises in your day-to-day life.

In the Trust Your Trust exercise below, you will begin to trust whatever it is that *your* heart, mind, and body are telling you to trust. You will begin to trust your Inner Feminine Power to make things happen in your life—and to bring you what you need and want.

Trust Your Trust

Begin by believing in your heart, mind, and body. Have confidence that they know the truth. Understand that you can rely on them to survive and prosper.

Look into your heart. What feeling is your heart telling you to trust? Love? Hate? Sadness? Pain? Gut reactions? Happiness? Take time now to listen to your Heart. (Pause.) Trust in the wisdom of the heart.

Look into your mind. What decisions, plans, or goals is your mind telling you to trust? A new job or career? Marriage? Adoption? Take time now to listen to your mind. (Pause.) Trust in the wisdom of the mind.

Look into your body. What responses is your body telling you to trust? Sexual responses? Good chemistry? Bad vibes? Take time now to listen to your body. (Pause.) Trust in the wisdom of the body.

The heart, mind, and body make up the Golden Triangle. Understand that trusting one part affects all other parts. Realize that trust is an Inner Feminine Power that will help you make things happen in your life and bring you what you want and need.

Trust Your Relationship

This is an exercise you can practice inwardly, when you are with the man in your life. We'll assume that a certain amount of trust has already been established. In this exercise you will learn more about what you trust—and don't trust—about the relationship. Trust is a strong bond between two people. But even if you trust the other person, there are very often things about the relationship you don't trust. For example, you may feel the relationship isn't going anywhere—that is, growth in the partnership is not taking place and the relationship is becoming stagnant. In this case you don't trust that the relationship is right for you. Or, in another example, you and your lover both feel that you need more time together. But you don't trust those feelings because time together will take away from the work that you love.

As they say, it takes two to tango. It's often unrealistic to expect the other person, by himself, to take the relationship where you want it to go, or to create an atmosphere of closeness. The relationship is a living, breathing entity and it exists, to a large extent, separate from the people who are in it. You can imagine the relationship as a large, beautiful house that is cared for by the couple living in it. While you may very well trust your partner, you also have to trust the house that holds both of you.

In this exercise, you will feel your trust and connectedness (or lack of it). You will begin to understand where there is love and trust and recognize where it is missing. The exercise is to be done inwardly, while you are with your partner in usual activities (eating, watching TV, hanging out).

Trust Your Relationship

While you are in the presence of your partner, allow yourself to relax. Let go of old habits, opinions, and preconceived ideas. Cast away stale mind sets.

Look at your partner and begin to feel your connectedness to him. Begin to feel what it is that you trust most about your relationship. Take time now to feel what you trust most. (Pause.)

Now, reach for something else that you trust about the relationship. Take time to explore this trust and the feelings that accompany it. (Pause.) Is there anything further that you need to bring to the relationship to strengthen this trust?

Begin to see what it is that you do not trust about the relationship. Reach for what you don't trust. Take time to explore what you don't trust. (Pause.) Acknowledge your feelings. Is there anything you can bring to the relationship to establish trust?

In the presence of your partner, open your heart, your love, your trust to the relationship. Feel your trust expand. Feel it widening. Feel it lengthening. Begin to find areas in the relationship in which to place your trust. Take time now to place your trust in new areas. (Pause.)

Many times when we set goals, we don't really trust that we can or will achieve them. It's sometimes hard to feel assured that our abilities will match up with our heart's desire—whether it's a challenging job, an interesting business venture, marriage, a home and family, close friendships, travel, weight loss, etc. Very often, there is something inside us that sabotages our best efforts. (Other times, we're just not in the right place at the right time, and life circumstances are not auspicious.)

Most often, goals are determined by the logically thinking mind, and unfortunately, feelings can be temporarily put aside. If your goal is to make more money this year, there may be very clear-cut steps to achieving what you have in mind. But your feelings have a viewpoint too, and you can trust them to inform you of what's in your heart. It is also possible for your heart to lead the way, and the money will follow.

Or, in another example, if your goal is to become involved in a love relationship, there may very well be a logical method of goal setting here (go out to social functions, travel, join a health club or a computer-users' group). But also trust your feelings. If going to parties seems like a sad attempt to capture a man, then trust your heart to inform you of how *it* wants to proceed.

The Inner Feminine picks up the sense of things as they *are* in your mind, heart, and body. It does not force experiences or circumstances into unnatural configurations. Let's say your goal is a career change. You've carefully thought out the steps you need to take, and you're working with a career counselor to actualize your goals. Despite setbacks, you trust that your goals can be achieved. You've learned to trust your mind and your abilities. But something inside you (perhaps a negative voice) doesn't really trust that anything is going to happen. And you've cut yourself off from *feeling* that your highest possible achievements can be realized.

In "Trusting Your Goals" you will begin to trust the *feeling* of wanting to realize your heart's desire. This is not empty-headed wishful thinking. It *is* making wishful thinking work for you as you go about putting your plans into action. It's very simply a question of staying in contact with your trusting heart as you go about the business of actualizing your goals. Some goals, such as losing weight, creating new friendships, or changing jobs, are short-term.

But others, such as marriage, entering a new business venture, or freeing yourself from substance and psychological addictions, can be long-term goals. Pursuing these dreams can be confusing and frustrating, and it's easy to lose trust in your feelings along the way.

We'll start here with a goal that you are trying to achieve. Let's say that you're trying to set up a successful desktop publishing business. Within a period of six months, you've gotten clients and work creating a weekly newsletter and an interoffice information brochure. As you go about your day-to-day business of trying to succeed, take a few moments to practice "Trusting Your Goals." Whatever your goal is at this time, begin now to trust the positive feelings that accompany the pursuit of your dream and let go of negative resistance that limits or prevents you from accomplishing all that you have set out to achieve.

The best-laid plans in the world will not be entirely successful unless your heart trusts them. In the following exercise, you will learn how much (or how little) you really trust a present goal. And you will begin to put your trust right into your goal.

It is important to note that beginning to activate trust in everyday life makes it immediate and alive. Whenever your Inner Feminine Power directly addresses your concerns (or others'), it becomes a vital force for positive transformation.

Negative influences are a constant in everyone's life. They surround us and they surface from within, seemingly to protect us. But rather than protect, they prevent us from going on with our lives and pursuing dreams of the heart. The word *pursuit* has been used here several times. It can mean chasing, hunting, and prowling. Or it can mean quest, desire, and intention. At its highest levels, it means you will trust the heart's quest, the heart's desire, and the heart's intention as well as those of the mind.

As trust in the heart's desire becomes more and more apparent and stronger, negative influences will become weaker and their power to control success or failure in your goals will diminish. The following exercise will help you observe your resistance to trust, and once observed, it can be dissolved.

The exercise below is to be done inwardly, while you are actively pursuing your goal. It can be done in a meeting, in a car or commuter train, at the health club, or even in the kitchen. Wherever and whenever you are carrying out plans to accomplish your goals, you can take time to trust your heart's intention.

Trust Your Goals

While you are in pursuit of your goal, give yourself the opportunity to relax your mind. For a moment, free yourself from tension. Begin to feel the freedom of a relaxed mind. (Pause.)

Take time now to look into your heart. Look at what you trust about your goal. Observe the positive feelings that accompany trust in your goal. (Pause.) Stay with the feelings of positive trust. Is there anything that you need to further strengthen this trust?

If you encounter resistance or negative influences from within, observe them as easily as you would observe a cloud. (Pause.) Then simply dissolve them.

Understand that goals are conceived by the mind and heart. Begin to feel your abilities and your desires as if they were one entity. Take time now to trust that your goal will be accomplished by unity of the heart and mind.

Trust Your Body

When you are sick with the flu, your body informs you that a bug has taken over and you become tired and feverish. You ache, lose your appetite, and want to sleep. There's a temporary shutdown of usual activities. Listening to your body, in this case, is obvious. You tune out until you recover.

But throughout a normal day, your body is getting thousands of messages that go by unnoticed because they are high-speed flashes of information just below the threshold of consciousness. These messages can be called subliminal when they penetrate the mind. However, the messages enter the body first, and when they become conscious, they can be interpreted by thought.

We couldn't begin to give credence to every message we receive, nor would we want to. But there are certain strong messages that are received over and over again in different experiences and situations. Let's say that every time you're in a situation of being put down, your body receives that message in your stomach (or shoulders, or throat). Or, in high-stress situations, your body receives that message in the space between your eyebrows (or groin, or the crown of your head). These repetitive messages are the ones that catch your attention.

Besides receiving messages, your body communicates messages, as all students of body language know. Whatever you cannot communicate—love, hate, jealousy, fear, anger, resentment, sadness—remains stuck in the body. It's fairly easy to tell when we are stressed, but sometimes it's not so easy to understand when we are afraid or angry. In some situations it is necessary to allow yourself to give in and trust your body to tell you what our mind and heart won't reveal.

When you trust your body, you also trust its power to heal itself, from both physical and emotional damage. No matter how much life has disappointed you or battered you about, take heart in the realization that your body can be experienced as a healing force.

In the exercise below, you will begin to trust your body to communicate messages and to heal its wounds. Trust Your Body is to be done while going about your everyday routine, rather than as a separate meditative practice. In the midst of normal activities, the exercise will teach you to become more aware of how trust and your body states and responses are synchronistically connected.

Trust Your Body

In the midst of your life, take time to trust your body to communicate whatever it wants to: joy, pain, anger, hope. Focus your awareness on the heart center and fully feel your body's message. (Pause.)

Trust in your body to heal itself of old wounds. Trust in your body to attend to the future in a positive way. As you go about your day, realize that your body contains hope and joy.

In this moment, allow yourself to experience your body as a healing force.

Last but not least, learn to trust in the universe. Trust that it will bring what is right for you. All the striving in the world doesn't matter a bit if universal forces don't cooperate. When you are depressed, frustrated, lonely, or disappointed, it is sometimes hard to believe that there are forces working to protect you, to help you realize your highest potential. Just as you trust in your own Inner Feminine Power and in the power of your Guides, now begin to trust in the power of the universe. It is not an abstract idea or intellectual concept. It is simply that you believe—given who you are—that life will present you with its very best possibilities.

9

Receptivity

When you are fully receptive, you are perceptive, sensitive, and clear. And you are open-minded, undogmatic, interested, involved, and open to suggestion. In this chapter you will begin to concentrate on evoking positive receptivity and on dissolving negative receptivity, if it exists within you.

We all carry the capacity to focus either on the positive side of things or the negative side. It's also possible to alternate between the two modes without being aware of it. When you mindfully and watchfully go through each day fully receptive to *what is there,* you can choose to emphasize and receive what is positive—and you can let go of all that is not. This does not mean that you repress or deny negativity; it means that you consciously discard it as easily as you would throw away a piece of rotten fruit.

To be receptive, by definition, means that you are open in much the same way that a container is open. But unlike a jar or pitcher or vase, your capacity to receive is virtually unlimited. The more you open yourself to your own inner resources and to the world around you, the more you can take in and utilize for the benefit of yourself and others.

To begin, it is necessary to create a heart space. In this place of power, you will receive every positive attribute that life has bestowed on you—whether that's intelligence, good looks, good-naturedness, an attitude of concern for others, a job you like, a loving friend, children, a husband or lover who cares for you, a comfortable home. At this moment, life has already granted you a series of wishes from, let's say, an easygoing temperament to curly hair or flashing dark eyes. You will begin, in your own time, to focus on—and stay with—what you have been blessed with. Whatever it is that you *don't* have—a more appreciative lover, a bigger and better house, more money in the bank, straight blond hair and blue eyes, thin thighs, a gregarious nature—is *not* received in the heart space. Whatever you don't have at this time and in this place is empty, null, void. Since it doesn't exist, it is a zero.

Desire will dictate whether some of these things actually come into existence in the future. Whether others come into existence will be determined by your situation and life circumstance, and still others will remain forever in the "if I win the lottery. . ." realm. But for now, let's focus on opening the heart space to receive the fortunate things life has given you. Positive receptivity is a powerful Inner Feminine Power. Once you understand how to open the heart space and receive life's gifts, you can go on to receive the gifts of others. Loving concern and friendship are just some of the gifts that you can receive in the heart space *when they exist*. It is easy to fool ourselves into believing these things actually exist when they don't. Very often we want so very much to believe that devotion or trust exists in a love relationship, or with a sister or brother, or child or parent. The will to believe can create an illusion of what exists, rather than mirror what is actually there. Remember, you receive *what exists* into the heart space. Whatever is nonexistent in your relationship is null and void . . . and cannot enter the heart space. (If negative projections or delusionary thinking take over your mind, it is important to be aware that you are not in the heart space.)

In time, as positive receptivity becomes stronger as an Inner Feminine Power that you can use in your daily life, more and more doors will open. As you begin to shift the focus away from yourself, you will realize that positive receptivity can mean listening to others in a new way . . . and helping others attain their heart's desire. By understanding what *is*—and letting that aspect enter the heart space—and by realizing what is *not,* you can transform the mundane into the magnificent. Balzac said that the more you look at something, the more interesting it becomes. The point, however, is not to become fixedly rigid by concentrating on what exists, let's say, between two people in a love relationship. It is to receive into the heart space what your lover is truly communicating, and stay with the feelings that accompany positive receptivity. The transformative nature of the heart space provides that whatever it contains will grow and become more interesting and positive the more you look at it.

In this chapter, you will begin, in the exercise called Positive Receptivity, with what is closest to you—your own unique qualifications to survive and prosper. If you're a fashion model you need full red lips; if you're a singer you need a song and a good voice to sing it; if you're a designer you need a good eye. These are life's gifts to you. Take time to give attention to your own unique gifts by receiving them into the heart space with conscious awareness.

You can do this exercise anywhere, anytime. It will help to center you in your own unique merits and enable you to focus on what you have, rather than what you don't. The benefits are especially valuable during times of disappointment, depression, or rejection. If you like, you can call upon your Guide to be with you while you are practicing the exercise. Simply evoke her presence and feel her nearness.

Positive Receptivity

Bring your attention to the heart space. Understand
that it is the container for positive existence. Begin
to focus on your blessings, the gifts that life
has given you. In your own time, receive
them into the heart space one by one. (Pause.)

Bring your attention to the feelings that
accompany positive receptivity. Stay with
the feelings. (Pause.)

Begin to feel your heart space accept
and be thankful for all that it has received. (Pause.)

If you become distracted or interrupted by
negative thinking, observe your thoughts as
they pass through your mind and slowly,
and with concentration, dissolve them. Return
your focus to the heart space and continue.

As you begin to experience positive receptivity in your everyday life, it will become less a matter of counting your blessings and more a way of centering yourself in them. As positive receptivity becomes second nature to you, opening the heart space will become an important way to deal with the joys—as well as the hassles—of life.

The potential for calmness, composure, serenity, presence of mind, levelheadedness, equilibrium, self-command, and poise exists in every situation and circumstance, no matter how turbulent. In the midst of a confrontation with a coworker or a lover's quarrel, the possibility for equanimity *does* exist. Imperturbability, unflappability, and tranquility are not generally what we are receptive to when things are flying fast and furious. It is definitely hard to keep the heart space open (even a bit) when you are defending yourself or protecting yourself from injury. But a positive receptiveness to serenity is possible even in the stormiest encounters.

Hatred, fear, and confusion are certainly things you can encounter and receive (from yourself as well as others). But you cannot receive them in the heart space, for this is the place of positive receptivity. When anger (or other negative emotions) rise to the surface in family quarrels, work situations, or between friends, the anger takes over and, like a demon, overrides any other possibilities for communication. If you're having a confrontation with your teenage son about his Saturday night curfew, it can be very easy to get into a shouting match, and in the process, not even think about positive receptivity or opening the heart space. In the same way, if your friend tells you that she's dating your estranged husband, jealousy, anger, and resentment could very well be your reaction. It seems hard to imagine how equanimity would fit into the situation.

In fact, when you are receptive to the heart space (and its

contents) *in the midst* of negative emotions (yours and/or others'), it can be a very powerful experience. Simply realizing that equanimity can exist, in spite of all the turmoil, can be extremely beneficial. Let's say you're in the midst of an argument with your mother. You feel that she's trying to control your life, that she's interfering and manipulative. Within you, there exists the potential to transform anger and hurt (which creates distance and separateness) into equanimity (which creats communion and connectedness). Whether or not you can transcend negativity is not so much the point. Success is not the ultimate criteria here. What matters is that you are *aware* that you can receive positive aspects of another person, of yourself, and the situation, and you can use those aspects to rise above the friction and tension that is pulling both of you away from the other.

Positive receptivity can be used at any time to bring energy from the heart space into the world around you. To do that, you must be receptive to the power that exists in the heart space—and its transformative aspect.

In Creating Equanimity, you will become more perceptive to the positive aspects of another person, of yourself, and the situation. The exercise can be done anywhere, at any time. It can be extremely beneficial when you are dissatisfied with the way your relationships have been going. In Creating Equanimity, you can choose to be with your Guide while you are practicing the exercise. Simply evoke her presence and feel her closeness.

Creating Equanimity

In the midst of activity, bring your attention to
the heart space.
Understand that equanimity exists
there as a powerful force. Begin to experience equanimity as a
calm and tranquil sea. (Pause.) Feel the waves washing away
anger, resentments, confusion, and fears. (Pause.)

Now, begin to open the heart space to receive the joy,
serenity, and peace that exists between yourself and
another person. (Pause.) Find the harmony that is part of

both of you, and experience its energy in your own
way. (Pause.) Begin to feel receptive to this harmonious
force that is part of all of us and unites all beings.
(Pause.)

In your own time, open the heart space by gently
breathing into it. Become more aware of your calmness,
composure, and equilibrium. Begin to bring poise and
tranquility into the present situation. (Pause.)
Be receptive and attuned to the power of gentleness. (Pause.)
Do not force anything, but simply allow equanimity
to be created between yourself and another person, in
the present situation.

Continue to remain centered in the power of the
heart space by gently breathing into it. Stay there for as
long as necessary.

Being receptive to others often means it is necessary to listen
perceptively, with an ear of understanding to what is being
communicated. Without becoming caught up in another person's
problem, it is possible to help someone close to you reflect on the
various aspects of her or his experience or situation.

While it is possible to have good wishes or another's well-being
or to send them joyful thoughts in a meditation, meeting one-on-one
is usually the most effective way to accept your friend's problem *as
it exists* (without denying any aspects), to see the positive and
negative sides of the situation, and with equanimity and happiness,
give positive energy from the heart space.

Giving energy from the heart space unconditionally will help
your friend find the tranquility and peace that is part of both of you
and that unites all beings, and it will help your friend find a
harmonious resolution to the problem.

Ear-and-Heart Listening, the next exercise, will prepare you to
listen—with your ears and your heart. In this way, you will become
more receptive to others' needs and desires. People are wonderfully
complex, and it's important to fine-tune the Inner Feminine Power
of receptivity so that you can respond from the heart instead of
reacting from the mind. Of course, Ear-and-Heart Listening also

prepares you to listen to joys and triumphs, as well as pain and suffering.

This exercise prepares you to listen to another person's concerns. Practicing the exercise before meeting with your friend (child, coworker, partner) is especially beneficial. If you want your Guide to be with you while you are doing the exercise, simply evoke her presence and feel her nearness.

Ear-and-Heart Listening

Listen with the Ear of Understanding. Stay attuned to the problem, as it exists. Accept the problem without denying any of its aspects. Acknowledge the positive and negative sides of the situation and the people involved.

Listen with the Heart of Compassion. Bring your attention to the heart space by gently breathing into it. Receive into the heart space everything that is positive and constructive.

Understand that listening with the Ear of Understanding and the Heart of Compassion brings greater clarity and responsiveness to almost any situation.

In this exercise, you will take in all that life has to offer, and you will give your love to all beings. Global Receptivity is a very powerful exercise because it brings receptivity and love into harmonious circulation. In time, as you become more familiar with the exercise and more attuned to its benefits, you can gradually increase it from two minutes to ten minutes. Again, you can choose to have your Guide with you by evoking her presence and feeling her near.

Global Receptivity

Bring attention to the heart space by gently breathing into it.

Breathe deeply and fully.
On an exhalation, open the heart space and, without
hesitation, take in all that life has to offer. On the exhalation,
give your love to all beings. (Continue for about two minutes.)

Receptivity is an active Inner Feminine Power. Extraordinary
forces are at work when you open yourself to whatever is positive
and life giving. You can encounter many different and complex
problems in your day-to-day life. Sometimes the answers are
simple; at other times there are no immediate answers; and often the
issues are murky. To penetrate confusion and lack of perspective, it
is beneficial to focus on a simple affirmation. The following
affirmation will help bring your attention to the active transcendent
power of receptivity:

> *Note:* "I am open to receiving positive energy and inner
> guidance. Each day, my attitude is becoming more open and
> receptive to positive change, and my life path is becoming
> clearer."

10

Inner Feminine Power — How to Get It Going

In the previous chapters you have been involved in a program that has provided useful information and ideas. You've come to understand more about your true feminine self, and you've participated in experiencing your Inner Feminine in new ways. Simply getting to know your Guides enables you to see the essence of your own femininity. And when you rediscover your true feminine nature, you can nurture who you *really* are. What more do you need?

To keep channels open and to keep new pathways to the Inner Feminine clear, it is first necessary to be aware of the active, transformative nature of Inner Feminine Power. This means that you are living fully and consciously with an understanding that *you* are the source and authority of your own growth and renewal. You have the power to pattern your life according to *your own* convictions of truth and beauty. You have the power to witness your experiences and relationships according to your own values. And you have the power to influence others with your strength, competence, capability, and love.

Secondly, it is necessary to *act* on the clarity that a connection to Inner Feminine Power provides. Rather than merely standing firm on your own inner truth, you can act on the courage of your convictions, fullness, strength, and power. Recognizing and valuing Inner Feminine Power is the first step. The second step is to make it work creatively in your world. It is a creative (and radical) act to transcend your own (and others') taboos and rules. It is also a creative act to make your way in the world, secure in your feminine energy. Being able to use your courage, imagination, love, loyalty, insight, resilience, confidence, and passion means you are able to use your power in human relationships. Often it is not enough to acknowledge and understand that you, for instance, are caring, empathic, creative, and intensely passionate. If they are not tested in day-to-day life, they can become abstract ideas rather than powers. On any given day there are many ways to be understanding, creative, and passionate. You can connect a lamp to electricity, but you have to turn it on to illuminate the room. In the same way, you have to activate Inner Feminine Power to illuminate whatever is confused or obscure—or joyous. And for Inner Feminine Power to generate transformative potential, it must be enacted.

There are probably as many ways of actualizing Feminine Power as there are women in the world. Each act of mercy is different; each tender kiss and each gesture of generosity is different from what went before or what will follow. But there are some basic guidelines that will help you each day to return to the source of your power.

When you read them, you may think that they are simple. They are simple in concept, but they're a bit more complex to follow as a way of life. Take each guideline one at a time and apply it to your life in a manner that feels natural and comfortable. In your own time, use the guidelines to help you remain centered in the strong and loving power of the feminine.

Inner Feminine Power— How To Get It Going

- Keep in touch with your Guides
- Remain emotionally powerful
- Feel that you are the directress of your world
- Look at what's right with your life
- Understand the locus of power is in the heart

Keep in Touch with Your Guides

Many issues and conflicts surrounding Inner Feminine Power can be resolved by means of internal dialogues with your Guides. They can help you gain access to your experience of feminine power (or lack of it), and they can connect you to your own inner voice. These Guides are images of your own empowering spirit, and they will remain with you throughout your lifetime. Never fear that they will abandon you.

Women today are entitled to images of women that empower the feminine spirit. For this reason, women telling stories of power, taking part in rituals, and celebrating natural cycles of change and renewal can also be used as food for thought and imagination.

Remain Emotionally Powerful

Always insist on validating the deep experience of your Inner Feminine Power. In plain terms, this means that you must never allow yourself to witness your power (or other aspects of your authentic feminine identity) through the reflections of another person.

It is only possible to create an understanding and realization of your Inner Feminine Power out of your own truth—not out of a man's idea of what that power should or should not include, and not out of a friend's idea, or out of society's collective view.

It's easy and sometimes flattering to let a man define your body image or your social function. And it can be satisfying to witness your self-confidence through a close friend's eyes. Or experience sexual pleasure through society's view of lovemaking instead of relying on your own values. When you can't or won't discriminate between your own truth and others', you temporarily lose power. It is diminished. When this happens again and again over a period of time, the meaning of your own love, anger, fear, and disappointment will become murky to you. It is only by keeping to the truth of your own experience that you can remain emotionally powerful.

Feel That You Are the Directress of Your World

You are the one that invents and constructs your world. You are the one that decides to revitalize and refresh your life by taking positive action and making the changes that are necessary for new growth to occur. If your feminine energy system is overloaded with work, social obligations, and family commitments, it won't be possible to even think about directing your world (much less explore your feelings about taking emotional risks and accepting new challenges). When you're busy reacting to life instead of responding to the power within, it is time to make time for contemplation and reflection.

At this moment do you *feel* as if you are the directress of your world? If the answer is no, remind yourself that you want to fully use your Inner Feminine Powers, and that you are actively waiting for the right moment to use them. Remember, you are empowered and entitled to construct and direct your world from your own perspective and experience.

Look at What's Right with Your Life

The "good life" does not necessarily mean a high-paying salary or a big house in the country. Learn to focus your attention on the *quality* of any given moment. Begin to experience a sense of time that pays attention not only to what is being done, but *how* it is being done.

When you begin to look at what's right with your life, shift your perspective. Isn't it more important (or just as important) to experience yourself preparing a meal with a loving heart than it is to strive for perfection? It is said that you can actually taste the love (or animosity, or anger) that goes into preparing a food dish. And how you talk to your husband (or friend, child, lover) is a part of what you say.

When you look at what's right with your life, look at the *quality* of it. Look at how you are expressing your Inner Feminine Power through genuine relationships. Look at how you accept nature's unhurried cyclic rhythms.

When you're rushing to the supermarket, running to an exercise class, dashing to the hairstylist, you may be caught up in achieving excellence. But is this hectic behavior a reflection of the quality of your life?

Looking at what's right with your life gives you a chance to focus on the quality of it—and to connect what you are doing with how you are doing it.

Understand the Locus of Power Is in the Heart

You reach into your heart to relate empathically to your partner, friends, and family, to express your emotions, and to nurture people you care about. Charity of the heart and gracefulness of the spirit are quiet, gentle powers. Do not underestimate them. Coping successfully with ongoing demands and being in control of your everyday encounters with life can be tackled by organizing, initiating, discriminating, and classifying—you can also deal with these demands and encounters by relating, accepting, receiving, nurturing, and creating harmony. When your behavior reflects the truth and beauty and essential worth of your inner feminine self, its power comes from the heart.

Be gentle with yourself. Be gentle with others. In gentleness there is great power.

11

Inner Feminine Unity

The quest in every woman's life is to unite her many different qualities into an image of wholeness. Even though these qualities may sometimes be opposite and contradictory, wholeness means a feeling of inner unity. It means that you can hold the tension between the different parts of your nature in harmonious balance. We saw, in the beginning of the book, how the Guides can be represented as six parts of a fan. The fan is a symbol of the spirit, of power, and of dignity. The shape of the fan signifies life, starting at the base and widening out just as the experience of life expands and fans out.

When feminine identity is formed in adolescence and young adulthood, certain traits, values, and personality characteristics are thought of as "myself." Whatever attributes are disclaimed are "not myself." So it's possible, for instance, to continue for years thinking of yourself as an achiever (a Kendra type) who's a bit of a loner (a Diana type). The "not myself" attributes of Eva, Nixa, Belinda, and Erika are feminine qualities that are denied. When you begin to identify more and more with this achiever-loner self (Kendra/

Inner Feminine Unity

Diana), and less and less with Eva, Nixa, Belinda, and Erika, it can create a state of emotional one-sidedness and imbalance. You can claim to feel unity, but this sense of unity is only partial, not that of complete femininity. Wholeness is lost when feminine attributes are unused. And Inner Feminine Power is diminished.

In the example above, let's say you fall in love and think about having a family. Earlier self-images have to be reconsidered as new self-images surface. And the previous pattern of self-perception changes. The Kendra/Diana self didn't dissolve, its influence will just be used differently.

Inner Feminine Unity is achieved every time you are able to pay attention to those parts of yourself that have been hidden, and you are able to use those qualities, if necessary, to test the waters of your new situation or experience. This is possible if you remain open and don't lock yourself into one dominant pattern of self-perception.

Inner Feminine Unity is achieved every time the different parts of yourself come into harmonious play and reach a consensus that brings with it a feeling of completeness, oneness, wholeness. Unity is a strong feeling of being "together," of acting out of the joint strength of your multilayered being.

Sometimes a sense of wholeness comes about effortlessly and naturally, but at other times it can elude you. It is possible, however, to create an atmosphere that encourages unity. You can experiment with what works best to restore a natural balance.

Stay fluid and flexible. *You* are the unifying force. You are the dancer and the dance. You are the power to bring together a self that is complete and wholly yours.

There are many images that are associated with unity. Since unity is a process of coming together and integration, it brings a sense of increased stability and reduced stress. The images of the circle, the pearl, and the symmetrical flower represent unity because they contain the idea of perfect form, balance, and harmony.

The image of a diamond represents the Inner Feminine that is indestructible and cannot be pulled apart.

Contemplation of these representations of unity can very often prepare the way for Inner Feminine Unity to occur. They are particularly powerful in times of great inner struggle, when things are literally "coming apart." The outer world and the inner world reflect each other. We all know how beautiful even the meanest street can look when you're feeling peaceful. Similarly, the most beautiful beach can look sinister and threatening when you're at odds with yourself.

Reflection upon a symbol of unity will bring with it the unifying force behind the symbol itself. This force automatically instructs us of its higher truth. In times of turmoil, this inner knowledge of the nature of unity can be reflected by appropriate action (or nonaction) in the outer world.

Here, then, are three representations of unity:

○ the *Circle* ◇◇

⊙ the *Pearl* ◇◇

❀ the *Rose* ◇❀◇

Each one is placed inside the Diamond—the indestructible Feminine. On the following pages you will be given contemplations for each of the images. You can read these to yourself, listen to them on a tape, or commit them to memory. The contemplations are to be used when you feel a need for a unifying force above and beyond the limits of your own personality and imagination. The images are expressions of the unity of life and they can communicate realities that are obscured or hidden from everyday consciousness.

In your own time, whenever you want a fundamental and effective way to achieve Inner Feminine Unity, go to the Contemplations.

The Circle ◇◇

The circle brings completion and fulfillment.
At its center, the Circle unites
wisdom, fear, knowledge, and hope.
Reflect on the wholeness of its perfection.

Contemplate the Uniting force within yourself.
Reflect on the wholeness of its perfection.

The Pearl

The night-shining Pearl unfolds
The power of the Feminine Moon.
The flaming Pearl unfolds
The power of the Feminine Sun.
Contemplate the Unity of the Moon Pearl
And the Unity of the Sun Pearl.
Reflect on the wholeness of its perfection.

Contemplate the Unity within yourself.
Reflect on the wholeness of its perfection.

The Rose

The Rose is the flower of the Feminine.
It is life, creation, fertility, and beauty.
Contemplate Unity within the five-petaled Rose.
Reflect on the wholeness of its perfection.

Contemplate the Unity within yourself.
Reflect on the wholeness of its perfection.

Epilogue

This book is based on our work with hundreds of women who have participated in the highly successful Feminine Enhancement™ Workshops. We've all laughed and cried together—and have asked ourselves important questions about our Inner Feminine Power. We've each made a lasting connection to our own potency. In our own individual quests, we found out that, no, we're not female eunuchs. We are our own power to create abundance, peace, and love.

Now we want to hear from you, dear reader. We want to know about your quest and about your path toward Inner Feminine Power. Please write and tell us, too, how our book has helped you along the way.

It is our intention to franchise the workshops in the United States and Canada. And we hope to produce a two-cassette and booklet instruction package.

If you want to write to us relating your experiences, and for further information on the workshops and tapes, please contact us at the address below. We look forward to hearing from you.

Dina von Zweck
Jaye Smith
P.O. Box #171
Peck Slip Station
New York, N.Y.
10272